THE PROMISE OF HOPE

African
POETRY
BOOK SERIES

Series editor: Kwame Dawes

THE PROMISE OF HOPE

NEW AND SELECTED POEMS, 1964–2013

Kofi Awoonor

Edited and with an introduction
by Kofi Anyidoho
Foreword by Kwame Dawes

University of Nebraska Press / Lincoln

Acknowledgments for the use of copyrighted
material appear on page 297, which constitutes
an extension of the copyright page.

This volume is published in association
with the African Poetry Book Fund.

Library of Congress Cataloging-
in-Publication Data
Awoonor, Kofi, 1935–
[Poems. Selections]
The Promise of Hope: New and Selected
Poems, 1964–2013 / Kofi Awoonor;
Edited and with an introduction by Kofi
Anyidoho; Foreword by Kwame Dawes.
pages   cm. — (African Poetry Book Series)
ISBN 978-0-8032-4989-9 (paperback:
alk. paper) — ISBN 978-0-8032-5493-0
(pdf) — ISBN 978-0-8032-5494-7 (epub)
— ISBN 978-0-8032-5495-4 (mobi)
I. Anyidoho, Kofi. II. Dawes, Kwame
Senu Neville, 1962– III. Title.
PR9379.9.A9A6 2014
821'.91—dc23   2013034296

Set in Garamond Premier by Laura Wellington.
Designed by Nathan Putens.

Dedicated to my children:

Sika, Dunyo, Kalefe, Tenu,

Afetsi, and Kekeli

that they may have a deep

understanding of who they are.

CONTENTS

FOREWORD

Kwame Dawes

That Kofi Awoonor is the first of what we hope to be an illustrious lineup of major African poets to be featured in the African Poetry Book Series speaks to several important things. The first is the way that generosity and a commitment to progressive struggle can open doors to important innovations. In this instance, the generosity belongs to Kofi Awoonor, who did not hesitate in saying yes to the request that came from the editorial board of the African Poetry Book Fund—namely, Bernardine Evaristo, Chris Abani, Matthew Shenoda, Gabeba Baderoon, and John Keene—to put together, on short notice, a monumental reckoning of his impressive oeuvre as a poet.

He said yes because he believed in the project of the African Poetry Book Fund, a relatively modest one—to publish four books of poetry by African poets each year. He said yes, I suspect, because he also recognized in the request a pattern of proactive generosity and literary activism that he has been at the center of for years.

Given his history as a great teacher, a highly regarded writer, an outspoken political thinker, and given also the fact that his reputation has been international in scope and impact, the editorial board of the African Poetry Book Fund agreed that he would be an excellent person to launch our new series. We all knew that we had to approach him because of how much we have all valued his work.

Finally, Kofi Awoonor is the first of this series because of the prestige, validation, and authority his presence in this series gives to us. He is one of a select group of poets from Africa whose body of work has helped to shape our understanding of African poetics and whose poetry demands attention.

This collection would not have been possible if his fellow countryman and the gifted poet Kofi Anyidoho had not agreed to work closely with him to put this book together. It took only a request by e-mail for Anyidoho to say yes and to achieve in a short period what can only be described as a remarkable feat—the beautifully selective and brilliantly constructed gathering of the best work of Kofi Awoonor. *The Promise of Hope* is important, also, because it constitutes the first major publication of poetry by Awoonor in two decades. He has, of course, been quite busy as a teacher, a diplomat, and as an important advisor to the Ghanaian government at the highest level for the past thirty years. Whatever progress Ghana has made in establishing itself as a stable and forward-thinking democracy over the past three decades is owed to intellectuals and committed leaders like Awoonor. Yet, it is a delight to know that during these years, he has been writing poems of power and profound insight, poems that we are now able to read and enjoy today.

This gathering of Awoonor's work seeks to ensure that African poets working today are able to recognize themselves as being part of a long and impressive tradition of writers seeking to find the language with which to articulate the distinctive experience of living on a continent whose ancient and current complexities remain ripe for the telling and the retelling. It would be wonderful to say that a collection of this nature is not an introduction to Awoonor for African readers, but alas one can't say this. One can say, however, that it constitutes a celebration of the work of one of our important world poets for readers both inside and outside of Africa.

ACKNOWLEDGMENTS

Many thanks to Mawusi Dzirasa, Keli Tsikata, and Israel Tordzro-Aguedze who helped to type the manuscript.

IN RETROSPECT | An Introduction

Kofi Anyidoho

Rediscovery and Other Poems, Kofi Awoonor's first collection of poems, was published in 1964 by Mbari Press in Ibadan, Nigeria. By a significant coincidence, *The Promise of Hope: New and Selected Poems, 1964–2013*, is being released in 2014 by University of Nebraska Press, the first publication in the African Poetry Book Series. In many ways, the new collection offers a unique opportunity for critical retrospection, a backward glance over a half century of Awoonor's distinguished career as a Guardian of the Sacred Word.

The collection opens with poems that point us in two directions, to a reconciled past and to a future of new challenges and new possibilities. First, to a past where we meet poet and country, young as the new moon and filled with hope and the promise of hope. We see in that past many memorials of struggle, inviting a stroll across a landscape of birds and flowers strewn with graveyards. But we walk arm in arm with the poet, with little fear of mortality. We hold our breath as the poet looks across a new dawn and introduces us to Death holding out his own "inimitable calling card" only to be ushered into

a homestead
resurrected with laughter and dance
and the festival of the meat

of the young lamb and the red porridge
of the new corn.

Here is a constant return to old familiar themes and subjects and the
need to postpone dying "until the morning after freedom." So we
find in "To Feed Our People" a gentle plea with the pallbearers and
mourners to hold back, just a little bit, while the poet persona attends
to a few outstanding concerns:

I still have to meet the morning dew
a poem to write
a field to hoe
a lover to touch
and some consoling to do
. . . .
I have to go [to India] and meet the sunset.

Above all, we must join the poet in "herding the lost lambs home."
Only then can we pass on to a deserved ancestorhood. The final lines
of this particular poem sum up probably the most important concern
at the core of Awoonor's poetry, from the earliest to the latest in a long
distinguished career: the duty we owe to our country, our people:

When the final night falls on us
as it fell upon our parents,
we shall retire to our modest home
earth-sure, secure
that we have done our duty
by our people;
we met the challenge of history
and were not afraid.

Despite the bold assertion in the last two lines, we find in his most
recent collection, "Herding the Lost Lambs,"[1] a constant return of the

funereal mood and voice so typical of the early Awoonor. As the poet himself acknowledges in "What More Can I Give?"

> I did not know it will return
> this crushing urge to sing
> only sorrow songs;
> the urge to visit again
> the last recesses of pain.

However, it is important to note a fundamental difference between the funereal voice and mood in these last poems and what we find in the early ones. These are not typical songs of sorrow. Rather, they demonstrate a mature reflection on life, a philosophical balance sheet carefully drawn to weigh life's gains and losses, with the final balance showing an impressive credit in favor of hope and the promise of hope. Through the thin mist of doubt, of uncertainty, we can see "a new beginning" in almost all the recent poems, as in "Up in the Garden," where in spite of tears that are still wet, the poet gathers "the courage of cobras" and surges on relentless, "each chronicle renewed / each earth reclaimed / each hope refurbished." His final victory, he assures us, "shall be recorded on a tombstone to be designed by my sons."

It is indeed, more than mere coincidence, that the first two poems in "Herding the Lost Lambs" are dedicated to Kekeli, the poet's youngest child, who arrived "one October day" "large-eyed, replica of the first / princess, and now the prince." The coming of Kekeli signals a victory over age and thoughts of death, a transformation of the long night of shadows into the light of a new day. Kekeli in Ewe means "light," hence the title of the first poem in the collection: "The Light Is On."

From the very beginning of a half-century career in the service of poetry, increasingly and indeed persistently, Awoonor takes us beyond the grave into the land of ancestors. With the earliest poems, especially in "Songs of Sorrow," the ancestors are called to order and even accused of neglecting homestead and offspring. The poet sends a direct query to Kpeti, Kove, and Nyidevu—all personal ancestral figures—asking why they idle there in Awlime while their offspring suffer and "eat sand" here in Kodzogbe, surrounded by termite-eaten fences, with strangers walking arrogantly over the homestead. This kind of negative homage is not unlike what we find in many traditional Ewe libation texts, where the ancestors are often reminded of the obligation they owe to the living, that if they expect their offspring to honor them with sacrifices and success in life, then they owe it to themselves that their offspring are blessed with long life, *with good health*, and of course some wealth.

Over the years, however, Awoonor's homage "to those gone ahead" has taken on much more positive and indeed laudatory attributes. Many poems invoke ancestral figures as a source of countless blessings and renewal of hope. And there are also the many poems dedicated to comrades in struggle who fell too soon, but whose memorials are the best testimony to a life led with profit, a life devoted to the resurrection of the best dreams of society. It is significant that *The Latin American and Caribbean Notebook* (1992) opens with the poem "In Memoriam," with its "single line honor roll":

> For friends gone ahead; Joe de Graft, Ellis Komey, Paa Kayper, Camara Laye, Chris Okigbo, Alex La Guma, Robert Serumaga, and Geombeyi Adali-Mortty, all the brothers who sang our song, and went home to the ancestors.

The poet's invocation of these comrades fallen in struggle ends with a promise of hope:

> we shall build the new cities
> over your bones,
> that your mortuaries shall become the birthplace,
> that our land and people
> shall rise again
> from the ashes of your articulate sacrifices!

Some of the comrades mentioned here were already listed among a long line of fellow writers celebrated in the earlier longer poem in homage to a leader among Awoonor's generation of activist writers, Ezekiel Mphahlele, in the poem "For Ezeki," published in *Until the Morning After*. The poem celebrates Mphahlele's courage in his decision to return home to an apartheid South Africa, even against a storm of protests from friends and comrades. Somehow, the poem manages to convey the long-exiled combatant's conviction that it was time to return home, that even as his own life was drawing to a close, he could feel the inevitable logic of struggle overtaking the arrogance of apartheid. At any rate, beyond apartheid, the call of home is a primal necessity:

> So you went home Zeke
> to seek memories along the goat paths, home
> to those lingering shrubs of childhood
> denuded by exile tears.

The need to return home to the soil that gave us birth is a mandate of nature we cannot deny: "We say / the snake that dies on the tree / returns home to the earth."

Another homage poem of special significance is "In Memoriam: Return to Kingston." Unlike "For Ezeki," "In Memoriam" is dedicated, not to a comrade still alive and staging heroic struggle against oppression, but to a lifelong comrade and brother now "gone like the furious wind of the hurricane month," Neville Dawes. Those of us who have had the privilege of listening to Awoonor speak again and again with love and deep respect for Neville Dawes understand why the poet had to travel all the way from Africa to Kingston, to be present at Neville's "furious homegoing," and why the poet grieves so much over this brother's death, and why, ultimately, his lamentation becomes a celebration. We note that Awoonor's novel *Comes the Voyager at Last* is dedicated, among other "extended family members of Babylon," to "the memory of my brother and comrade Neville Augustus Dawes who revealed to me the miracle of story time, and gave us hope for liberation."

In many ways, this relatively long poem becomes a series of snapshots of countless times spent together in combat as in revelry, in fields of struggle and in memorial halls of fragile victory, recollections of significant stages of a long journey from

> slums and cold tenements
> on urine-wet floors of tram-ways
> . . . .
> across snowfields
> fired on storm nights
> of blazing friendless territories of exile
> and exile tears.

We hear the poet weep anew "for historical follies I could not shed," but soon, we watch him smile in memory of toasts drank "to struggle with the people" and of

> meals we shared
> at early sunset or sunrise
> in smoke-filled rooms redolent with conspiracy
> and strategies.

At final countdown, we are not surprised to witness "the doors of Babylon closed again," this time behind the poet and his comrade and brother, "with Neville and I on the freedom train, / going home, yes, going home."

As we step back in time from one collection of poems to the preceding ones, we find a constant return to and variations on old themes, but we also follow the poet on a return voyage away from those narrow shores of childhood into an expanding universe of exciting vistas of new and newer worlds, each with its own agonies, its own fields of sorrow giving way to monuments of struggle and victory and promise, each new world with its own history of endless human possibilities. Once, we listened to the poet as he heard a bird cry again and again in agony over fallen homesteads of his birthplace. Now we follow the poet and eavesdrop on his jubilant songs as he imitates the joyous calls of mating birds on that almost mythical Isla de Juventad, the Cuban Isle of Youth.

The Latin American and Caribbean Notebook occupies a unique place in all of Awoonor's collections of poetry. Written during and out of the poet's sojourn in Brazil and later Cuba as Ghana's ambassador, these poems bring us farthest away from homestead and country only for us to discover that our steps are constantly treading not only new and unfamiliar territory but also replicas of ancestral grounds filled with memories of historical injustices and monuments of struggle. Some of the faces we encounter in the streets of Montevideo, Rio de Janeiro, Kingston, and Havana could have been those of kinsmen and women back home long gone into the shadows.

Another early fruit in Awoonor's garden of poetic delights that matures into full bloom in *The Latin American and Caribbean Notebook* is the poet's constant dwelling on images drawn from nature—his constant reference to specific animals, birds, trees, flowers, rivers, and, above all, the lagoon and the sea, the land, the soil. If ever we are invited to a festival, it is most certain to be the festival of the new corn, ripened with the golden rays of the sun and mellowed with the silvery shine of the moon and stars. Most of our journeys are over the land, not on highways or boulevards, but on bush paths through thorn fields, with occasional stretches of salt flats and flower fields. Sometimes, we journey by sea, by lagoon and river, often in leaky boats. But the boatman and oarsman are unfailingly dependable, their gaze on a final destination constant. Even when the boatman happens to be Kutsiami, Death himself, we have no fear of disaster, knowing that we will land safely on a shore bustling with familiar ancestral faces, a welcome festival waiting for our safe return home.

The abundance of images of nature we find in *The Latin American and Caribbean Notebook* may have been reinforced by the fact that Awoonor's childhood love of nature found fulfillment in the wonderful opportunity to pursue his old hobby of hunting, especially in Cuba, that magical island with a landscape that inspires even as it intimidates with relentless hurricane seasons. But we note as well that even from prison, that house by the sea, Awoonor's poetic imagination is on constant lookout for snatches of nature's reassuring presence as he peeps through the tiny window and catches the swift flight of a seagull, or the sun's rays retreating beyond the horizon only to give way to the a rising moon, even if only a half moon. Wherever we look in his poetry, Awoonor's love of nature is constant and provides occasion for some of his loftiest poetic statements. But this deep love of nature is always connected to a deeper love for social justice:

> I know a paradise
> when I come into one
> of an evening over a hill
> on an island
> when mountains crouch like lions
> and rivers are threads
> soaked in the hero's blood
> deep dyed in a many tears. ("The Hero's Blood")

And if the poet is never incapacitated by thoughts of Death, it is because he knows for certain that "where the worm eats / a grain grows" ("Across a New Dawn"). The promise of hope so briefly, pointedly captured in this recent poem, was already there in an early one ("The Gone Locusts," in *Rediscovery*), where the poet "watched the locusts / From the east come in clouds; / And then the tops of the trees were no more." But rather than break into ululation, the poet invokes his

> wish for the return
> Of the sowing season
> In which the farmer
> Will remember his harvest.[2]

In another early poem, "The Weaver Bird," one of his most frequently anthologized pieces, Awoonor portrays the weaver bird as an archetypal colonizer, who came and laid his eggs "on our only tree" and ultimately destroyed the tree, desecrated the sacred shrines, and took over the house, indeed "preaching salvation to us that owned the house." Again, significantly, the poet spares little time for cursing, for lament. Rather, he insists on inviting the comrades to a determination to repair the damage done, lest it becomes a permanent disability: "We look for new homes every day, / For new altars we strive to re-build / The old shrines defiled by the weaver's excrement."

Perhaps, it is this unfailing anchorage in hope that seems to have seen the poet through probably his moment of greatest stress, political imprisonment without charge, and for a long time without trial, as recorded in *The House by the Sea* and in a few recent poems. Of all of Awoonor's collections, *The House by the Sea* is perhaps the most challenging to read, to fully digest without a lingering sense of discomfort. Even in part 1, "Before the Journey," in poems mostly written in Awoonor's final years of exile, there is a sense of brooding disaster hanging in the air, despite the obvious sense of anticipation as we count the days toward the inevitable return to the native land. There are too many reports of killings, political assassinations, and Death, "the removal man / reaper-angel of profaned destinies / locks the door and hides the keys." Miraculously, the land endures, but there is some sad reckoning to be done, as we seek in vain the passionate pleas, the voluble chants of Pablo Neruda, now lost to a reign of terror,

> when Ugarte with his cohorts
> slit the throat of Salvador Allende
> in the name of American liberty
> and you [Pablo] had to die.

In America, the poet could not rest easy:

> Between the sun and my head
> a pen of blood rests to write the story
> of Negroes hanged in Jackson

black boys shot in Memphis
. . . .
The guns still patrol the streets
for Law and Order.

And back home across the Atlantic, much of hope goes up in flames as thunder rumbles through the land: "Wole in the Nigerian jail / Okigbo in flight to the musical burst/ the last dance of our drums." In the midst of all these heartbreaks, the poet embarks on the homeward journey out of exile, from his own account, a return journey made by sea, by choice. The poem "Departure and Prospect," most of it written on the Atlantic voyage of return, is one of the most memorable in the entire collection. It opens with a pledge to country, to self, and to Mother Earth:

Seven years, and I'd like
to care for the dying,
clean sores in the iodine mornings
on tropical grasslands and scapes;
I'd like finally
to start the foundations of my dream house
Smell again the pubic groin
of my ravished earth.

Against this noble declaration of plans, most of the poems in part 2 of *The House by the Sea* read like a sad reversal of the poet's best intensions and fortunes. The poetic voice itself comes and goes in brief, fragmented statements, sometimes of historical facts long forgotten, sometimes of enduring fond memories of loved ones, often of recurring and lurking dangers to self and nation, evil men dressed in camouflage as revolutionaries with sinister designs. Even the final poem that closes this collection, "The Wayfarer Comes Home—(A poem in five movements)," one of his longest, is generally devoid of the bold declarations of hope we encounter in most of his other collections. The poem opens on a note of personal and collective tragedy:

Even here in my cell
in the house of Ussher
I hear the guns
They are killing the children of Soweto.

And it closes with little promise of hope, as the poet confesses, "I will have no trophies to show." Of course, there are many hopeful moments in *The House by the Sea*, such as in poems like "On Being Told of Torture," but such moments are too quickly overshadowed by the brutal reality of life in prison, presided over by fellow citizens who are ready to torture you to death, as they did to Allotey, one who had died earlier in the cell now occupied by the poet, as they almost did to the poet's brother and comrade in struggle, Capt. Kojo Tsikata.

In a prison yard they crushed
the petals of our being
against a long row of ancient walls and
a line of assorted flowers.

This memorable juxtaposition of rare beauty and immeasurable pain is redeemed, a few lines later, by probably the strongest affirmation of hope in *The House by the Sea*, lines so lofty that they provided the title for Awoonor's comprehensive selected poems, *Until the Morning After*: "So much Freedom means / that we swear we'll postpone dying / until the morning after [freedom]."

Until the Morning After: Collected Poems 1963–1985 (1987) has the distinction of being selected as winner of the Commonwealth Poetry Prize for the Africa Region in 1986. Except for the last nine poems grouped under "New Poems," the entire collection features most of the key poems from Awoonor's first four collections, namely, *Rediscovery*; *Night of My Blood* (1971); *Ride Me, Memory* (1973); and *The House by the Sea* (1978). The nine poems listed here as "New" seem to belong to a period of meager harvest, most likely the transition between Awoonor's American years and his return home in 1975 to a land trembling under considerable stress and deprivation imposed by a military dictatorship best remembered by many for its nervous reaction to dissent, with the generals and their hangers-on freely looting the national treasury and growing prosperous in an economy marked by a proverbial scarcity of every conceivable "essential commodity." Considering the poet's stand on the side of dissent in a time of repression, it is not surprising that most of these poems reveal a mind constantly haunted by premonitions of death. His fears were soon to take concrete form in his arrest and detention without trial in an old slave fort still filled with the constant smell of death:

> Along a hope hill and fields
> when dreams crush like petals
> . . . .
> We move on, carrying I say
> a singular faith in death
> the only companion in this valley. ("Life's Winds")

Against this image of a bleak world dominated by constant thoughts of death occasionally relieved by an instinctive faith in the eventual, ultimate order of a free and just world, the very last poem in the group and indeed last poem in the collection, "For Ezeki," stands as a powerful monument to revolutionary struggle anchored in the firm belief that every soul lost in struggle shall not have died in vain. As we wait "For the coming excellence of days / For the lovely resurrection time," it is crucial that we remind the young ones not only of a past made proud and memorable by heroic struggle against oppression, but also especially of a future beyond looming catastrophes of a present life ensnared in death and dying:

> Above all Zeke
> tell them of hope and the promise of hope
> encrusted beneath death
> and death's tears.

of the excellence
and the vision
that no perfect armament can destroy;
of the human will that shall endure,
of the coming festival of corn and lamb
of the freedom day that shall rise
as the sun tomorrow.

Of Awoonor's *Ride Me, Memory*, we may take note of the following critical observations made in an earlier essay:

A remarkable change occurs in Awoonor's poetry in his third collection, *Ride Me, Memory*, mainly through a widening of the thematic and stylistic range of his poetry. There is no clean break with earlier preoccupations. The dirge mode and style, for instance, continue in the final section, "African Memories.". . . But *Ride Me, Memory* as a whole, moves away from the lament into other areas of the oral-poetry tradition and into artistic traditions outside Awoonor's immediate ancestral heritage. . . . The work is a testimony to the commonality of human suffering, struggle, and aspiration, compelling a celebration of various successes, however small. Quite understandably, Awoonor displays deep sympathy for the experiences of the African peoples of the diaspora, incorporating several lines and themes from African-American literature and music into his poetic sketches.[3]

These observations must be seen against the background of the main trends found in Awoonor's earliest collection, *Rediscovery*, and especially in the more comprehensive *Night of My Blood*. The widening of thematic and artistic range noted here must also be seen as a logical outcome of the poet's travels outside his homeland into the wider world of human experience. His initial entry into the United States, following his sojourn in the United Kingdom, coincided, significantly, with the unfolding historical drama of the civil rights movement and with the rising heat of the Cold War as well as the Vietnam War. The impact of these world-changing events on the poet's expanding consciousness and artistic sensibilities is very effectively captured for us in part 1 of his 2006 collected essays, *The African Predicament* (Accra: Sub-Saharan Publishers). A brief return home during this period, which the poet used to conduct field research into African oral literature, eventually saw the publication of two of his most valuable scholarly works, *Guardians of the Sacred Word: Ewe Poetry* (New York: Nok Publishers, 1974) and *The Breast of the Earth: A Survey of the History, Culture, and Literature of Africa South of the Sahara* (Garden City NY: Anchor Press, 1975). In both works, Awoonor provides a rich scholarly demonstration of the unique Ewe tradition of *halo*, songs of abuse. But even before these two works were published, Awoonor had already drawn on the tradition to write his own satirical songs of abuse, as seen in *Ride Me, Memory*.[4]

Awoonor's literary career provides a significant instance of various ways in which the critical insights of the research scholar and the creative impulses of the poet-novelist offer mutually beneficial influences on each other. Indeed, some of the earliest critical statements about meaningful ways of reading aspects of Awoonor's early poetry and those of some of his contemporaries, especially Mazisi Kunene and Christopher Okigbo, may be found in Awoonor's work as a scholar. The principle of creative continuity between African literature written in colonial heritage languages and the rich heritage of African oral literature is now a well-established fact, but a coherent critical demonstration of this fact was a relatively new and still-contested notion prior to the publication of *The Breast of the Earth*.

Awoonor's early poetry, presented in *Night of My Blood* and *Rediscovery*, attracted a great deal of critical attention and quickly secured for him a place of honor among Africa's leading poets of the twentieth century. Some of that criticism may be found in a very useful bibliography compiled by Kwaku Amoabeng and Carrol Lasker, "Kofi Awoonor: An Annotated Bibliography" (*Africana Journal* 13 (1982): 173–214). A useful update is provided in a major bio-critical essay published in *Dictionary of Literary Biography*.[5] In the essay, Awoonor's very first collection, *Rediscovery*, is considered "remarkable for its confident handling of metaphor, thematic consistency, and pure lyricism" (117:81). And *Night of My Blood* is praised for its firmer grasp of style and technique, its sense of increasing urgency, and especially the deployment of a special technique of "the collage" in the handling of a wide range of historical and contemporary events and experiences.

> Ezekiel Mphahlele in his introduction to the original Doubleday edition of the collection, describes such a style in terms of a musical medley. . . . At one level, Awoonor pulls together themes, images, lines, and line sequences from several of his earlier poems. At another level, he draws on a baffling range of apparently disparate and fragmentary experiences, historical, mythical, or purely symbolic. All these scattered bits are then pasted onto a wide canvas and are held together by a coherent rhythm and movement, the essential unity of which is sometimes registered in certain basic thematic lines repeated in a carefully regulated pattern. The poems in which this technique is best seen are necessarily long, among them "Night of My Blood," "I Heard a Bird Cry," "This Earth, My Brother," and "Hymn to My Dumb Earth" (117:84).

A close reading of much of Awoonor's poetry, especially the first three collections, is certain to profit from another dimension to his versatile literary career, his autobiographical work, as seen in some of his essays, but especially in "Kofi Nyidevu Awoonor," in *Contemporary Authors Autobiographical Series*.[6]

In the epilogue that closes this commemorative selection, the poet himself declares: "This is the source of my poetry, the origin of my commitment—the magic of the word in the true poetic sense. Its vitality, its energy, means living and life giving. And that is what the tradition of poetry among my people has always meant." We only need to turn to his elaborate autobiographical essay, to see how firmly his artistic vision is rooted in the ancestral soil and soul of his heritage, but with the liberty to travel far afield for the exploration of other essential dimensions of our common humanity.

The very last poem in this collection, "Songs of Sorrow," is included here for the first time in any Awoonor collection. Although it is perhaps the one poem by which generations of lovers of Awoonor's poetry best remember him, he has never put it in any of the earlier collections, in due recognition of and respect for Henoga Akpalu Vinoko, the best known of Ewe oral poets and the single greatest influence on Awoonor. As explained by the poet himself, "many of [his] early poems are built around central thematic lines directly translated from Akplalu." In the particular case of "Songs of Sorrow," the entire first segment consists of a translation of lines from two well-known Akpalu songs. The point of "creative continuity" emerges, especially in the closing segment, where the young poet does honor to the older singer by using his craftsmanship as a model to draw directly on his own family history to elaborate on the ancestral story began in the songs of the older poet, Akpalu.

It is this ancestral story of sorrow and of ultimate victory over sorrow especially in the death and resurrection of Hope that the young Awoonor took up half a century ago and through various creative transformations and adaptations as he traveled around the world, the now statesman and elder Awoonor has brought the old and changing story back home in the voice of the sage and Guardian of the Sacred Word, inviting us to join hands and minds and souls as we Gather the Lost Lambs Home. We welcome our long lost kith and kin back to the ancestral land and to a harvest of powerful images, of sun, of moon, of thunder, of lightning, drums and trumpets, and of course dance, in the company of fellow humans from all corners of Earth, joined by all creatures of the Earth—an amazing Festival of the Word, appropriately captured in a vintage Awonoor prose poem that closes his novel *Comes the Voyager at Last*. In this final entry, we pay homage to Kofi Awoonor not only as a poet with a profound vision and articulation of the world, our world, but also with a gift of words that is at home in poetry, in prose, in critical literary studies, and equally in major essays about our African, our human condition.

NOTES

1. This collection was put together for release in 2003 as a bilingual text, with English and corresponding Ewe pages facing each other. But the publisher/printer made such a mess of the final product that the entire project had to be abandoned, and the copies printed were never released for distribution.
2. This reference to the coming of locusts could have been inspired by the poet's recollection of a major plague of locusts experienced in his birthplace in 1939, an incident still cited today in oral history.
3. Kofi Anyidoho, "Kofi Awoonor: A Bio-Literary Essay," in *Twentieth-Century Caribbean and African Writers*. Vol. 117, *Dictionary of Literary Biography*, ed. Bernth Lindfors and Reinhard Sander. (Detroit: Gale Research Inc., 1992): 77–92.
4. Kofi Anyidoho, "Kofi Awoonor and the Ewe Tradition of Songs of Abuse (*Halo*)," in *Toward Defining the African Aesthetic,* ed. Lemuel Johnson et al. (Washington DC: Three Continents Press, 1982): 17–29. Reprinted in Richard K. Priebe, ed., *Ghanaian Literatures*. (New York: Greenwood Press, 1988): 87–102.
5. Anyidoho, "Kofi Awoonor: A Bio-Literary Essay," 117: 77–92.
6. "Kofi Nyidevu Awoonor," in *Contemporary Authors Autobiographical Series*. Ed. Joyce Nakamura. (Detroit: Gale Research Inc., 1991) 13:29–54.

THE PROMISE OF HOPE

From *Herding the Lost Lambs* | 2013

POEMS IN ENGLISH AND EWE

The Light Is On

A gray pigeon has just flown in
across the green country
where loafers chase a speck of white

How I used to
adore the summers
the windswept landscape
the open fields
and the lush foreboding country

Ah I almost forgot the water
wide wide as the vistas
of youth, the wish to curb a
foreboding future full of formidable
prospects receding now so fast

Each gnat is part of this inexorable
universe, this inevitable landscape
with its own inimitable echoes.

Our journey, supported by time and wind
captive of a May morning
away from the original March heat
when the shimmers over the water
glimmer so fiercely.

There are times when a new sorrow rings
when regrets, palpable as obvious fruits
of ill-considered acts
without hidden agenda
loom large as fate

Dear dear sorrow
rings, reminding, just reminding
of a time ahead, not for reckoning
but only for recalling as fate.

the time we as young as
our country
dreamed of obvious success,
of achievements measured
in concise yardage
of promises delivered,
of children protected from age,
the time
when the river from which we came
shall sweep us along
toward the original source
of eminence and glory,
when we will defy love
and death,
when we shall stand
by the beloved country as the single tree
struggling to be a nation
and a forest

benevolent fathers,
when we forget the loins from which we came
nudge us back into the river,
send us up the same water
by which we came

so with the last fish
we can cross the last ocean
to be one with the fire that
warmed your feet

guided you over deserts
by pyramids and temples
shrines and sacred groves,
on that island
where once the bird
was plentiful and the hunt
was good, and the cheer
was loud and the laughter joyful

and ah! the child Kekeli
came one October day
large-eyed, replica of the first
princess, and now the prince
has come promised
someday, by some river
I shall teach him the
last light and reveal
the divine affair
of which he is part
of which he is an heir.

here is water for your feet
here is flower for your feet
here is wine for your lips
here is the embrace I promised.

The New Boy on the Block

He came one October night
screaming blue murder
out of a swearing mother
whose enormous pain
disarms, hurts
mystifies

Away from the antiseptic smells
and the silent steps of the attendants
waddling across a vast eternity
of a delivery hall
I waited for your arrival.

A small music flows
across time
reminding of another birth
at another place

I swear that I shall stand by you
that I shall prepare the field
for your planting time
provide the seed
for your sowing dawn.

I shall raise my tomb
a full memorial for your
wondrous future
so that wherever I fall
you shall rise up.

At an age

when many rock themselves
into an easy chair
I chose to father children
and to hell with who disagrees
including the lobby against birth
run by eunuchs and fools.

Welcome, boy, you have come
to sweeten the falling years
when leisure is less than planned
and romance blooms in the eyes
of a lovely woman.
Hurrah for fatherhood.

Fair souls that canter
across a golden era
of crowns and gravestones
delicious hours of long lost
love and the brevity of faith
in the infinite certainty
that God exists
and loves all His children
without exception
assures us

I dreamt again that dream
of childhood,
this time I left the homestead
walked across a small dune
cactus filled a row
erect, arrogant beyond belief
and the claim they
are the remnants of divine action
which fools ascribe to the first man

The fear of the grave
is real
I still shudder
passing by cemeteries
particularly those planted
with the curative nim
and the forget-me-not
winds howling by
among stones shabbily laid
by masons whose sense
of size and measure
confound the sharpest eye.
Builder, king, queen
Sun-god and priest
Of my temple

Good Lord, Whatever
the price let me pay
it in the full knowledge
that your mercy rests
secure, and You and Your host of
deities shall be with your son
and your people.

Across a New Dawn

Sometimes, we read the
lines in the green leaf
run our fingers over the
smooth of the precious wood
from our ancient trees;

Sometimes, even the sunset
puzzles, as we look
for the lines that propel the clouds,
the color scheme
with the multiple designs
that the first artist put together

There is dancing in the streets again
the laughter of children rings
through the house
On the seaside, the ruins recent
from the latest storms
remind of ancestral wealth
pillaged purloined pawned
by an unthinking grandfather
who lived the life of a lord
and drove coming generations to
despair and ruin

But who says our time is up
that the box maker and the digger
are in conference
or that the preachers have aired their robes
and the choir and the drummers
are in rehearsal?

No; where the worm eats
a grain grows.
the consultant deities
have measured the time
with long-winded
arguments of eternity

And death, when he comes

to the door with his own
inimitable calling card
shall find a homestead
resurrected with laughter and dance
and the festival of the meat
of the young lamb and the red porridge
of the new corn

We are the celebrants
whose fields were
overrun by rogues
and other bad men who
interrupted our dance
with obscene songs and bad gestures

Someone said an ailing fish
swam up our lagoon
seeking a place to lay its load
in consonance with the Original Plan

Master, if you can be the oarsman
for our boat
please do it, do it.
I asked you before
once upon a shore
at home, where the
seafront has narrowed
to the brief space of childhood

We welcome the travelers
come home on the new boat
fresh from the upright tree

Songs of Abuse

I once swore to forgo
the abuse songs, the dirge
and the praise poem for
straight verbal statements
direct comment and simple talk
as fresh as the child's language
before comprehension

But I have enough provocation
to renounce my oath
and return to cursing the night
the falling light
and the inglorious criminals
whose ancestry stretches to
the fornicating hard-arsed baboon
and the smelly hyena
who laughs as he feeds
on the corpse of his grand-aunt

I know you all, you
products of thieving jackals,
stepsons of frauds
who rechristen themselves
donkeys believing it is
a higher-sounding nomenclature

I know you all, you lascivious brutes
I know one in particular
his mother an aging whore
his putative father

a lunatic criminal
with a record of political molestation.

And the congregation of contumacious rats
who in concert with products
of unions between calculating whores
and a race of swamp goats
now perched on a pedestal of power
visiting on the beloved republic
the shame of their mediocrity

I will spew out the venom of years
expurgate the hurts of one generation
so that I retain my sanity.

I love the after-harvest fields
when the wild hen roams

I denounce your arrogance
your false claims to virtue
and your monkey ways

I challenge you to prove
you were not fathered
by a barnyard sheep
and an errant baboon
who it is established
was raving mad.

That you found money somewhere
to print a newspaper
is not a mystery
every fool with a fool's tale

can coax money from other fools
for ignoble purpose

But the fact remains
that your mother is still a whore,
your father, well
some said he took a Bible
into hell, babbling obscenities,

the simple fact is
he was a certified lunatic,
part of the destructive howling winds
that rocked the sanity of men.
how expertly you mimick him

To Feed Our People

Do not dress me yet
lift me not
unto that mound before the mourners.
I have still to meet the morning dew
a poem to write
a field to hoe
a lover to touch
and some consoling to do
before you lay me out.

Has the invitation come yet
from India?
I have to go

and meet the sunset
share time
with the Florida pigeons on that Island,
I have to meet again my friends in Agra
where they owe me
for pictures and a memory.

Why are we not calving the cows
or herding the lost lambs home ourselves?
Why must we think
others will lead our horses
herd our sheep
and feed our people?

We must bring in our harvest
father the children
and thatch the barns.
We must build the roads
clear the paths to the planting fields
and clean the holy places;
and oh, we must meet the
morning dew wet,
work with the early sun till the vertex
when it will come home with us.

Then after the wash, then only
shall we bring out the drums
recall old glories
and ancient pains
with the dance our dance.

When the final night falls on us
as it fell upon our parents,

we shall retire to our modest home
earth-sure, secure
that we have done our duty
by our people;
we met the challenge of history
and were not afraid.

To the Ancient Poets

They said they found a strange
woman at my door
one deep night

A messenger indeed from the gods?

The gone befores,
I call you again,
I call you, Akpalu *akpa, gogowoduto*
Bibia bi wofoe na woviwo
I recall our last encounter
by the lagoon shore on a breezy cloudy day
when the rusty roofs of Keta
had disappeared in the mist;
gulls, in an early gambol
across our lagoon
recall the shrieks
heard since time
coinciding with your voice
proclaiming "I shall go
beyond and forget"

your songs were the sons
you bore; you sang;
the rain beat you
the sun scorched you
the firewood of this world
is not for all
that is why you did not
gather it.

Dzenawo, *nyonu gbade*
a woman of high worth
you sang the dirge of wealth
and death
the eternal stalker
who plucks the young
and leaves the old
refuses gold
and insists on man,
who harvests the fields
he did not plant
who locks the door
and hides the key

and all of you,
those gone ahead
into the long night of life

My ancient friends Dunyo,
mesea gbagba o,
Komi Ekpe
who said his deity
is stuck in a brass pan.
You stood by your gods
and went home a holy man.

All of you;
take a message to our fathers
to Nyidevu, *medaa ke vu o*
to Afedomeshie
the black beauty of the ancient

Vuyokpo, you who left recently;
what did I do wrong
for you to leave in my absence?
Why didn't you wait for me
to bring the eye drops
you ordered
and deliver the iron bed
you asked for?
Why?
But you were only an errand woman
sent to the old ones
to deliver our long-spoken message
Gbe Kuetrome, I recall you now
how swiftly you left
I recall our rich sessions
when you spoke of Kofi Wodi
and his traveling friend.

Welcome, this is where we are
at home with the termites
the hour will surely come
so let us be ready.

Counting the Years

As usual, as in the earlier dreams
I come to the whistling shores
the voice of the high domed
crab stilled
but a chorus remains of the water creatures
of earlier times, of the birth time
and the dying time, the pity,
when we resurrect the travelers
the anchorman on our singular boat
that will take us home

Once More

I came again to the whistling shore
the wind lashing the gray trees of the after-rains
across my usual bay
where I ran a race as a boy
the thorn bush wept for the squirrels
bereft of nuts in a season
when the palms refused to ripen
and the wine turned a thin sap
unequal to the task

how weary I am
of the need to do good
cheer the weepy
and comfort the sorrower:
what more strength can I summon

for this miraculous effort
at mercy?

An ailing tree
reminds us of a journey
to a far-off kingdom
of the man, unalone
who hanged they say
for all

I believe still in the unity of man
in the sun rising tomorrow
in the rain to grow our crops
in the gods and the ancestors
in infinite grace and mercy
and the ever-presence
of the Divine force
who gives to all HIS/HER children
without fail
without discrimination

On the Gallows Once

I crossed quite a few
of your rivers, my gods,
into this plain where thirst reigns
I heard the cry of mourners
the long cooing of the African wren at dusk
the laughter of the children at dawn
had long ceased

night comes fast in our land

where indeed are the promised vistas
the open fields, blue skies, the singing birds
and abiding love?

History records acts
of heroism, barbarism
of some who had power
and abused it massively
of some whose progenitors
planned for them
the secure state of madness
from which no storm can shake them;
of some who took the last ships
disembarked on some far-off shores and forgot
of some who simply laid down the load
and went home to the ancestors

Truth

I watch the countenance
of this man, looking for the tell-tale
signs of truth, honor, fortitude
and a faint whiff of gratitude
only a wry smile
eyes on the verge of blazing
a terrible effort to dissemble

alas dear gods, he gets away
with it

What Brought Me Here?

What brought me here
is more than the desire
to share a common fate
partake in the work and promise
of man and country

What brought me here
is the determination to heal
the thorn-wounds
of those with eternal miseries
and the burden of night-time cries,
of orphans without meals
of lepers without fingers
of holy men without faith

Dear God, what consolation
have you stored for us
after these fretful days
in the service of ingrates and wickedness?
How much pain shall we endure
as our hope burns in chains
beside the hanging tree?

O how little
is our faith
in an eternal deity
who lashes our souls
with sin and the promise
of redemption

I caught history's eye

the other day.
I saw the anguish in his eyes,
as I watched his life-lines ebb away
I smelt the fear on his fetid breath
as time wound itself
in the final sheets of an ending.
I remember not the hour
of regrets, pain, and sorrow
but the time when I
was young as the new moon and nation
on a clear June evening;
wrens and the cuckoo dove,
the one that keeps the hour
on our savannas
sang a jubilee
"all that is not given is not lost"
why must thanklessness
cover the tail of work done,
commitment so ably made?
my friend the Methodist
in answer to my query
proclaimed,
"God is His own interpreter
and He will make it plain"

What More Can I Give?

"if they do not heed my call
I will walk alone"
A lifetime used in service
at times at the behest of saints
and heroes, at times, only at times

at the behest of not so good men
and women

So much does my infant's cry mean
so much, my friends.
Returning once along my favorite road
homeward, beneath a crazy bridge
occupied by bats
hearing a siren crying
a fellow to the sick house
I thought I needed a pee.

The fact of our lives,
full of achievements
vilification, praise
or contempt from those
who surely do not measure
eternity becomes a quotation
posted on the billboard of a single life.
Passions are exhausted
love, renewed again
and again
to satisfy a basic longing,
journeys made, departures recorded
deaths foretold again
and again

I have the fear that I am not done
that my gnat days will be long
tedious and melancholy
the premonition that not much
will come from the vigil and the sweat
and the tears and the long hours
and the sacrifice

That I come from illustrious men
and women is an obvious fact
but also that in this gene
I harbor not so good
men and women, persons
of questionable morality and obvious flaws
is no matter

I did not know it will return
this crushing urge to sing
only sorrow songs;
the urge to visit again
the last recesses of pain
pluck that lingering hair with a wince.
how long shall my God
linger in a brass pan
the offertory unreceived?

Those Gone Ahead

I dreamt again this recurrent dream
of my father
taller ever than he has ever been
in the dream
I traveled on the seventh night
to Awlime, the land of spirits
to visit my people,
those I know and those who know me

On a mat in a corner
under a shady Gbaflo tree
lay my sister Comfort

A bit leaner, her beautiful
smile, frozen by death
as radiant as ever

Oh, how I recall
her capacity to turn
an insipid rabbit
into a festival of delight
the lowly partridge seared
in the oils and onions
of the field
her generosity of spirit
stamped upon her willingness to give
of herself
large and relentless,
kindness was her middle name

When the night fell on her
her startled eyes
of inquiry, set upon me
and I, helpless as the leaf
in the storm
could not save her
nor give answers
to her terrible questions

I believe a love
died here some years ago.
Across a bay I can
hear the distant music
haunting, sweet remembrance
of good happy days
of innocence hung in a bar
at Osu;

of the girl who fainted in my room
out of sheer joy

There is surely a living time
when the recollection of death
slightly shudders
especially when I remember the
burial ground
where the house now stands
among mimosa and nim.
the second gnarled
the first tender
as the first day
the second the companion
of death and dying
sinewy, arrogant, persistent

Truth, long my friend
does not deny
and ah, what matters
the despair, the disaffection
of this engagement
when liars, bums
ambitious mountebanks
and certified crooks
short on memory
and basic decency hold sway.

They say misery it is
who acquaints man
with strange bedfellows.
In my case it is not misery.
When I die, I believe
the sun will rise

the morning after,
radiant;
it could be wet
in the afternoon
a cool breeze
meandering through the trees
regular;
what will they be saying
when I am gone:
quite a bit;
that I was a son of a bitch
arrogant, intolerant

But I shall go
perhaps to seek the lost rest
roam the wide vistas
of my afterlife.
savor the welcomed
boredom of eternity
where they say the skies
are pure blue,
and rivers never run dry
and the day lingers on
and on and on
and no one hungers
after food or righteousness

Will I see loved ones
gone ahead
relatives and kinsmen?
I expect the boatman
will carry me over
without a fee, my companion and minder
on the road to the place of rest

Up in the Garden

Through a thin mist
and a light silhouetted
across slightly swaying trees
reminding of a far place
I see another beginning,
a mess of trees neatly arrayed
by the Master's careful hand.

My spirit soars
this May morning
through a chill
I had fought
the last hour
from a damp bed
in a filthy room for hire on a hill
not far away.

I am here
on the edge of the green country
nursing a pain
gnawing immense immeasurable
perhaps a bit of fear too,
an apprehension for a life wasted
doing things I should not have done.

Although many have gone
and the tears are still wet
I gather the courage of cobras
and surge on relentlessly
each chronicle renewed

each earth reclaimed
each hope refurbished.

I pledge
that my palm trees still prosper
so thirst cannot be my death
and victory shall be recorded on the tombstone
to be designed by my sons.

Xiansi, Pou Tou Dalla

I returned to the People's Republic 16 seasons
long after the storm of the Cultural Revolution
long long after the Long March
when faces, after crossing
the Tatu river
smiled
Beijing is a new city.
by the gates of the Forbidden City
the crowd is thick;
drawn from every corner
of a new world;
Americans, overburdened with wealth
and guilt; Japanese short-stepped.
with cameras and an equal guilt.

The compass that guides this earth
swings on the mercury point
a clear blue spring in Dalian
against a perfect blue sky
on a China day.

China is no longer on its knees.
In Pou Tou we spoke
to the party secretary
he outlined poverty programs,
"we gather
to bring in the harvest
and plant the new wheat
for the three disabled families" he said.

How does China survive
after the papacy of Watja
and the historic presidency
of Reagan, and the grip
"of the Iron Lady
womei Yao hepi
wimei yao tuuli."
The early summer days
in Xiansi, tours
in the Chin and Tang dynasties;
the terra cotta troops
are marching near my window
on the road to unite the tribes;
the horsemen and archers
forgot their haversacks
so they'll sack the villages tonight
for wine, women, and dance;
the small orchestra
trails behind the troops
torn flags and songs
float amidst dancing birds
and leaves and rain drops

China is awake
Let her stand
and be counted

let China speak
on the crimes against
the victims;
let China speak against oppression
crime and pain
Let China tell
that the Revolution
is not over,
that the festival of the oppressed
has entered a new phase,
new suns once arisen
are struck down by the historical criminals.
But China, more than a Sun
shall blaze shower
its lightlets
on a weary world
Arise Ye Starvelings from your slumber
Arise Ye Prisoners of Want.
Merciful moments
raindrops on cactus leaves
pear on the road to Xian
and a pause at the tomb of the Empress who poisoned her
granddaughter for a gossip

China once burdened under the demons
foreign devils
dragon kings and warlords
1901 saw the war of the devils
1911 was the year of Sun Yat-Sen
1949 was the arrival of the Red Army
which feared not the Long March

In the Summer Palace
we sailed on the lake
by a wide row of

peaches and pears and pelicans
A late spring rain fell on us,
in little showers
tender like the gnat's wings
sparkling against a suggestive light
in the throes of a rising wind.
The dragons, the devils, and the demons
have been exorcised
Mao, Deng after many leagues
of the Long March from Hunan to Beijing
arrive at the Gate of Heavenly Peace.

I'll Raise a New Song

I burst a vein
plugging each hole
in this leaky boat
in favorite hour
when laughter and tears
are one
prepared as I am to endure.
I hate hypocrites
and fools;
the latter I could say
are God's creatures
but the former
are the devil's apprentices.
Seascapes I knew
as a boy repeat their shapes
as I stand upon the shore.

The million moths
my sister and I chased
no longer come
to the open field
which I cannot locate.
We are the children
of the hills through which run
the slow river;
the siblings
of the savanna lion
and the leopard
who still lingers in the forest.

I have seen the sad
and fading light
of many evenings in many lands.
I have heard the echoes
of unfamiliar birds at dawns,
the howl of the coyote
and the bark of the mountain baboon.
Sorrow was a witness
my companion for so long.
Yet I am ready
to raise a new song
a war cry
for freedom anew.

The iodine smell of the sea
the fragile fragrance
of the wild lily
evanescent, illusionary
a little undesirable wind of a July night
forgetful of the April heat

and the oppressive barometric height
confirm, as you reflect
on your immortality.

You, sir, have been a witness
to the immense drama
of time and space;
you must give evidence
of this immeasurable beauty
and God's majesty and mercy
He who out of the simple
clash of cymbals drums
and percussion agents they say
created the universe
and gave the cosmos
a gift to his most transient creation, man.

You, the king of this nutshell
the eternal audience
participant in this drama
who will come again and again
Till infinitude and time and space are filled
full with the eternity of God's mercy
which shall endure they say, forever.

Remembrance

I saw a man on the farm road
yesterday chasing the lines
of last night's rain
his eyes wet
with wake-up tears
recalling a long sorrow
a familiar ally of many
family tragedies
and endless sorrows

I pause near a young logo for relief
a scrawny partridge crossed
from a newly harrowed
field waiting for the planter's hand.
We watched it
lost in the safety of a shrub

Each road I walk, dear gods,
must lead to the fine home
you promised.
My sorrow nurses itself
for a happier time
a festival of lamb and corn
a time of endless dancing

Solomon's mother was a whore
and I will tell her son
when we meet
at heaven's gate
because he was named
after a wise man.

Solomon's foolishness
shines like the evening star
radiant, and loud

The universe began
our folks say with a bang
when the Thunder God visited his wife
then song was born
the mother of the speech
the dance and the wail
for the final trip

The world is music
open your ears wide
and listen
you bunglers
religious idiots
and moral cripples.
A bird that falls
to earth is not necessarily ill;
it is only
charging its energy
drawing from the affine rays
that nurture the force that puffs
the green leaf
over a thousand miles,
that blows the storm
that brings the rain.
So a time for
sustaining the souls
through goodness hereafter
and the promise of bliss
in a land
not too far

where the mess of seasons
does not occur

And the sun shall be suspended
by the original charge of goodness
so we can see God face to face.
I'll crush a rat
and settle a score
at God's behest
reducing to ashes the nascent seed of a new dawn
My memory suddenly recalling Medellin
and the clean city of Invicada
settles in a corner of history, waiting,
just waiting

Through the green garden
of my house
I watch the main rain come
in little drops, season by season
marking alas . . . the time
when I draw nearer
to that perfect understanding
which may perhaps be granted
beyond the clay
and the grave

From *Latin American &*
Caribbean Notebook

In Memoriam

For friends gone ahead; Joe de Graft, Ellis Komey, Paa Kayper, Camara Laye,
Chris Okigbo, Alex La Guma, Robert Serumaga, and Geombeyi Adali-Mortty,
all the brothers who sang our song, and went home to the ancestors.

This single line honor roll
weakens, sags, yet longs
for the heady exhilarating hour
of friends and comrades.

Some visit irregularly
like Joe who points out
all the stars in the brightening firmament
to a mumbling recitation
of one recollected evening.
Today Israeli soldiers killed a 3 year old boy in
Gaza for throwing stones at military vehicles

And who said that the drama of the dying
wipes out the consequences
and the central theater of death?

Brothers, your tombs are the verses you carved
on granitic memories;
oh, how I grieve over the tempests
that blew away the young poets
singers of all our songs in this land of fetters.
We promise we shall build the new cities
over your bones,
that your mortuaries shall become the birthplace,
that our land and people
shall rise again
from the ashes of your articulate sacrifices!

Of Home and Sea I Already Sang

Of self too, the intimate details
of creeping age,
the sudden surge of gray,
the uncertain bone, creaky now underneath
a hip, slightly projecting a limp
the Japanese lady in Sao Paolo
said it made the right longer
than the left.

A calm settles
at the beckon of sweet age
and love is sweeter
than the waters of *paraiso*.
Joy and hope soar
for the ultimate task
ahead written about, already
promised in the trajectories of jail,
in absence and exile
envisioned in the immaculate seer's dice.

That we will perform our duty by the people
depose the recalcitrant brutes
and march ahead of our beloved masses
to a coming kingdom.
We have claimed reprieves, honors
vacations, like Sisyphus on leave from his legendary
boulder heaping upon heads long shorn
grains ground by uncertain teeth
threatened by the unsuspecting mint.

I am the circular fire unquenchable,

the drum that plays for the rulers of the earth.
"Kings and Kingdoms shall pass away,
but my benevolence shall not pass away,"
once said the preacher.
Grains ground by the pimply professionals,
for pain, let's postpone the meeting time and set
another hour
near dawn preferably,
when calm and dew shall besiege the world
and night tears shall have long dried.

Today the Americans shot down an Iranian civilian
plane over the gulf of Persia. 290 people including
60 children perished.
President Reagan said it was not his fault.
The fools have closed the western bridge again
So I have to drive around a bend
beyond the lake
past the eucalyptus at sentry
past the waste treatment factory
with the signboard advertising
achievement in stench-control
by the squatter community perched near a ravine
where an accordionist plays
old forgotten sambas without audience
along the superb dual carriage way
to the club to drown my loneliness.

Let the dream not die, master;
Let the dove coo at dawn again,
Let the masthead rear its head
out of the storm
and share the night with me on this sea.
Let me sing the song you gave me.

Before death comes, master,
Let me dance to the drums you gave me.
Let me sit in the warmth of the fire
of the only native land you gave me.

Brasilia

Of Home Once More

I love a land
in minuscule tear drenched
in misery; but hope
shines on its shores
and denuded hills;
come a time when this love this passion
will not be let die
on thorny fields home or away
but nursed by hope's other sister
fortitude whose strength is the amazing
good for the installation of grace.

Calm now as I steady my boat
for the far but cautious shore;
loves lost, friends dead,
and the refuge in an inane occupation
to keep sanity, receive orders from fools
and pompous jackasses
in the agony of the beloved country
as the dreams we dreamt are rent apart
in ill-considered conduct
where once, love, brotherhood

and faith in the wisdom of the people
blossomed.

I steady my nerves for try
in the soon to come time
when we'll regather the people
for the meal of smoked partridge
around the oblong table of our father.

Soon will come the time
when thru tears
we'll glean the hills
washed clean after the rains
cascaded down our hearts
aches stilled at noon
a time for flames and swords
for arms and strategy,
for victory
        or death.

Rio De Janeiro

Fearful and Lovely City

Indicate a ship
for us to sail to the mimosa fields
through Ipanema, Guanabara
the bay the idiot Portuguese sailors mistook
for the river of January;
small arms industries
bronzed girls in the briefest shrifts
sailing across the crystal sands of a crippled city

blowing *beijos* to the passing world
marooned in hotel rooms on Copacabana
secured by guards
and a whipping wind.
Down in the lower regions, out there,
beyond the glare of the July sun,
the fruit-peddler hums a tune
to an ailing guitar
of love, pain, and absence
of hunger and race despair
in this possible and abundant country.

They come to the fiesta across sand dunes;
the limping habitants of inconsolable *favelas* bring their
music to the *carnavale*
proclaiming that rhetorical *alegria*
they say came from Africa;
infinitude, and plentiful harvest,
co-scavengers roam in bandaged feet,
black and inexorable as my race;
a distant drum beat
the glaze of the light of the primal journey.
On which shores have they landed
on which shores?

The singer was with them
new tuned his descant
rising above the threnody
tremulous like the drums of the afterharvest
across once vast ocean front of home
now shrunk, oh, shrunk
to the sandstrip of childhood memory
marked by the covenant of graves and the cross
brought long ago from Bremen

Oh, sing again my people,
join my song of sorrow, of pain and agony tainted
occasionally with a little joy
that was the signal and the badge
the amulet we wore on this battle ground,
the talisman of our hope and endurance.

Suddenly I feel that surge of age
in a flood of memory of an adage
of survival, struggle, fight, and victory;
I feel like doing all the women as I puff my graying chest
pump my muscles into a bulge
and date the enemies of all my days.

I come again, the braggart loudmouth boastful
uncertain diplomat
after a long season
crafting an answer for the prosecutors
as the Rio de la Plata splashes outside my window,
a lingering southern winter wind
caresses my bones chilled ahead
by the night without sleep in Rio
in a bunkered room they call Luxor

Montevideo—same walk same wall
same old men angling for the shit-eater fish
in the brown murky flow of the Plata.
An idler asked me for time,
mocking once more my negro head
as happened once in B.A. Alex and I.
Each angler clutched his rod.
Two old drunks embrace.
One detaches himself and calls
"Ben Johnson"—the Jamaican boy

who won the 100 km in Seoul and,
wrapped himself in the maple leaf
only to lose the diadem
in an accusing hall of shame. I smiled back
I stop by an antique books store
Staring at tides
—rare birds of South America
Fly squalling in Spanish, French, and Portuguese
Not in Guarani or Quechua—
a negro staring at rare books in Montevideo
of rare birds.

The 8th day of spring, yet again
another walk, a last acoustic jaunt
across the listening aqueduct
panoramic sea front—
a palpable negro was pissing against a wall
facing the atlantic of his ancestral home.
Beneath the wall was the legend
"Viva la droga
el sexo e los pena";
the poet forgot to add "la muerte."
There was the incrustable tablet of stone
to Bob Marley *el rei de losoltitos*

I retraced my steps
sad now a little
a setting yellow sun now little
in a half-dip curtesy to the Plata;
the gulls had settled for the night
the negro was drinking his last forgettable
glass of sorrow's wine.
By the locked church I walk, sad a little,
pass Theatro del Solis promising a Brecht tonight

across the *plaza de la independencia*
columns palladian as a Greek's nose,
my last walk perhaps in this city
on this side of this century

Rio—Montevideo. September, 1988

Distant Home Country

I appropriate rivers
hills, and lakesides,
seashores used to be my home
in a distant country,
now a narrow strip only
of childhood
memory. I am
rivers and floods
in the ravaging land
of the old continent
and the young country
of tomorrow.

I came to the gate
on an afternoon
before the burial;
mother sat as usual,
in her little casual corner crumbling
near the charcoal stove
ready to cook
all our meals,
sad as always,
mother.

"When I die" she said one noon,
"I wonder whether you will all come
to an empty house."
I played with gods when a boy
took them from Sofe
to the open fields and rivers;
One in particular, elongated head
an enormous member erect,
a god of jokes mischievous as a god
winking at all the perfect pranks of a boy
executed under his charge,
my god, my friend,
to orchard raids, preaching
simple morality to a little boy
in a god and a people's name.

Then I saw Death dancing one noon
with the English lady
with the nasal twang acquired in Adelaide
They danced on the asphalt
outside the winter hotel
on the cold east shore
of the river in that strange city
whose name I cannot recall
at this point of the last sun they danced.
A gull dashed across a bay
where once a sick child drowned dashed,
shrieking.

Agra

January 21, 1989

A pearl,
what I record here
is merely dust
against the red of the fast
and the eastern glare
rising is the mystery of the Taj
in its majesty.

After Agra,
along the dusty road jammed—
with cattle and men,
memory holding the door now
as I contemplate
the sun and the dust
across a bay recalled again
the Taj Mahal in splendid arrogance
Jihaadists in bows across,
in the imperial mosque
I saw the prophet dusty from the desert
searching for a tree to tender his aging camel.
All the footwears of the Islamic nations
placed in rows on spiritual pavements
I record here now, this India,
sad monstrous
     magnificent India,
Remember is the gift of the gods
May Allah give us life Allah Akbar Akbar! Ami, Ami.

Cuban Chapters

Santa Clara:
    Written in red and fire
across the soul of this little island
whiffed with pimentos
and scents of burning cane fields
in barrels of tears and rum.
Jose to Fidel, Che
Camilo Cienfuegos
the many heroes of the vertical hills,
carriers of hope once sealed
in the claws of the northern eagle
once hidden by the fury
of the stripes and banners,
now unfurled in one single starred-bandera
    of freedom!

That evening in December
the wrens came home to roost;
overhead a stormy wind blew
the distance without horizon
laid out beyond recall.

30 years ago, they came here
Che and his brothers;
30 years he stands here tall
after the fall in Bolivia
in the company of iron comrades
who hammered down mountains
smashed boulders and rocks
to re-channel rivers and seas;
around his head now a halo

on his face a vision
in his hand a gun, in his eye a love supreme
    a love supreme.

The Hero's Blood

I know a paradise
when I come into one
of an evening over a hill
on an island
when mountains crouch like lions
and rivers are threads
soaked in the hero's blood
deep dyed in a many tears.

I came carrying a lamp
to see the face of the gardeners
now resting under a *logo* tree

Then a wren came
    fluttering
        seeking respite
from the hunters from the north
the purveyors of righteousness
and death;
I seek a reprieve
from the hunters from the north
the purveyors of righteousness
and death;
I seek a reprieve
from the judges

to bring the herbs missing
in paradise.
We cannot die
until we give account
of the freedom day
that shall surely rise
as the sun tomorrow.

Of Faith and Fortitude

On paved seas
and clear blue and liquid marbles
granitic souls of non-believers
shatter the peace of innocence,
in our teeth we hold
firmly unto the bird
in flight, feathers furled
gay bright comrade
of this incontestable choice
to feed my people

And God shall be with his people
This Hopi prayer haunts me still
two decades ago in a far country;
faces of comrades,
many dead now
return to the verge
of personal disasters.
Palms, the tall Cuban variety,
Marti's symbols of men
Martial replicas of the vertrix

of hope
raised on my native ground
seven years ago;
and God is with his people.

The Orient Express

When the poet went to India
January 1989

He had never fought shy of truth when it was dangerous; nor made
alliance with falsehood when it would be convenient.
Rabindranath Tagore on Nerhu

That night in Delhi
across a marginal street
strewn with strollers
a loud brass affair came
playing an indeterminate tune.
The groom looking slightly lost
in a horse cart; his relatives nodding to the music
as they led him merrily to the slaughter
far on the northern end of this city of dreams.
The police agitated officious like hens
happy for a procession
tossing their night sticks.
Ernesto Cardenale was having his birthday
64-revolutionary poet priest humanist
Combining love of God with love of man.
Agnus Dei qui tollit pecata mundi
Ora pro nobis.

The horses nervous and doped
dance on the midnight air;
soon they vanished beyond a copse;
the hills shade them from us.

Betrayers

They planted a dream
My ancestors—in this unselfish gene
self mutilated
     to weep
For those who have not
     share not
For the power men and their brokers
insatiated automatons
of unfeeling worlds
civilized agents of death
horses wizened into second fiddlers
in a vast defeaning symphony
of universal hate.

That I am a nigger is no matter
but that I continue to die
in Memphis, Ullundi, Soweto, Maputo
and Harlem offends my self-esteem—

Their hate, I say, stacked with certainty
even against their mother and birthplace
denying the very feel of the eastern wind
the very torrent of love and pangs
that delivered them.

They copyright their sick geniuses
in inane poems and self-promotional essays
seek shelter under imperial roofs
citadels of lies and evasions,
more lies compound
their betrayal of our race our land our corn our people.
That was the day the Bombay boy wrote a book
the believers said blasphemed the prophet—
May Allah shine his countenance upon him—
The Ayatollah in his mosque at Qom
pronounced a death sentence.

Then all the hypocritical money-lovers
the historical assassins and conscientious slavers
destroyers of forests and hills
the sackers of cities and homesteads,
plunderers and pederasts
organized a hysteria—
and with the support of the empires dead and new
they beat the drums of war against "terrorism"

I cradled my queen
warm she is my love,
oh memory
she whom I left on the far shores of a river
weeping inconsolably.
The mid age love
to fill a chilling gap
between hemlock and hyssop
between tears and tears
evening dreams wired
in strings of sweat
in an empty alien bed
in an alien far city

I am learning to tie my knots
to pull closer this dispensing wind
to make corporate
this body of my intimate god,
ancestral as memory
tied to many faces now
in anonymous burial grounds
in the now-distant birthplace.
I will crush a million mountains
and foothills
flatten cathedrals and temples
to make room for fields
to plant corn for the people

This kingdom where I stash
a memory
green as the remembered home
with the sheep-eye tree in bloom,
the putrescent corpse
in the bush-rat's home
carried aloft by a sad-faced lone murderer
in 43, so long ago

"an abandoned hospital in South London became
 a temporary shelter
 yesterday for a few of the
 city's estimated 30,000 homeless
 people" writes Peter Murtagh
"Free soup . . . ."

Mrs. Thatcher balanced her books
issued statements on human rights
in Poland, Czechoslovakia and
declared the breaking up of a riotous assembly

of dissidents in Prague
"unacceptable to her Britannic Majesty's Government"
The Black youth of Brixton, Manchester
and the wounded cities of the north wait,
The Irishmen of Ulster in jail houses
and in freedom's graveyards wait, wait
for human rights, democracy, and free speech.
"an abandoned hospital in South London be-
    came a temporary shel-
    ter yesterday for a few of the
    city's estimated 30,000 home-
    less people . . . ."

Give us this day our daily bread;
in our father's house where
the mansions are filled
with texts of how books were balanced;
impressive statistical data
on the 9th year of economic growth
"an abandoned hospital in South London be-
    came a temporary shel-
    . . . ."

Havana, Cuba

The Free Territory of the Americas

Arriving in Havana December 1988
I search, I search
the features of the dare
the audace and righteous anger
of Marti's children;
the paling graying stepsons of Antonio Maceo
he who rode to battle
with a creaky press;
am searching researching
looking into the faces of the horsemen on the plazas
for the weaning convex metaphor
of death and bravado
in the graying strands of Fidel's beard
he who without saddle or horse
stands taller than Marti's palms
or the remnant pines of Isla de la Juventud,
he who fused the original dream
with the certain vision of youth
dared the eagle in his abominable lair,
wove the red haloes of victory
around the guerrillas' sacred heads
and crested victory or death in rainbows
formed by streams of blood
and the cane-cutter's sweat.

I walked Havana
searching for the men of my village.

I saw them all, saw

the gray old boy with the toothy grin
the mischievous brat with the ample laughter
the buxom girl-bride singing to her child
a long recalled lullaby of the ancestral home;
ah, this brother, with his morning rum
and that, oh, coming sister with erect nipples
and the inscrutable smile of my original hills.

I stretch a hand
across 450 years
of prenuptial night raids
and slave-ships, whips and tears
to you who bore the cudgel scars of my iniquity,
the shame and infamy of my senseless indifference,
you whose tears well and
fall over my eyelids
as I leaf through the book of degradation;
I swear, I beg of you, I swear
I too stood with you on the auction block
I stumbled with you on the inevitable paths
across marshes and observant forests;
we heard the dogs together
as we hid in the futile caves of trembling;
we heard the clamor of continuing comrades
the din and wail of the brothers
left at home on the African plantations.

From the bowls of cane juice squeezed
from the bones of our mutilated comrades,
we drank a toast to death and exile.
We wept, oh, we wept deliciously,
we wept rivers redolent of the clan and the ocean
that brought us here.

Havana, Havana, how sweet the name,
in the mystic silence of equinoctial nights
recalling struggles—only struggles;
I return to the Isla de la Juventud
renewed by the vigor of foreign youth
all from home—the black remnant continent;
I am still to go to Santiago, Camaguey, Matanzas
to go again to Santa Clara
where el Che stands towering
stern defiance etched by the sculptor's infallible chisel,
Che, who lives in the memorials of a Bolivian death
and a Cuban victory.
He speaks, of victories in death not
the dearth of victories,
of struggles, always *siempre* of struggles.

Oh memory, please bring me back to the rivers
I forded, the fields I tramped;
Bring me back, oh, to the village
crush me an orange
bake me a clam
dressed in my favorite peppers
grill me a fat snapper saused
in herbs of a thousands forests
served tenderly of an evening
near the palms, a swaying moon witnessing
by my favorite woman, mother
mother, sad-eyed long betrayed by a careless husband
father, self-taught hero
of all my personal tragedies,

Come all of you gone ahead
defiant heroes of a furious fate
at home and abroad

come eat with me this vertical memorial
testament of our collective harvest
swear with me the old oath
that we cannot thirst
when our palm trees prosper
our rivers fish filled
our corbs grained
by He who sends rains and storms
steadies the winds for our determined sails
on a sea mapped for the battle,
he who loves all sends us farthest afield
to recount the mysteries of his hand

A Caress

So I hang my head
not in shame
but in polite withdrawal
from battles I cannot lose
in the silent impulse
that swats the fly
the gentle touch that weaves
itself a caress
the holding hour of the lover-girl.
of all my days, oh,
she as sweet as the apple-pine
lyrical as an angel
in that village whose name I do not recall
straddling hope
for a better country.

Resurrect all my dreams, my fathers
so I can dream them
for the new people who are coming.

Mortal I am as a little Kingdom
redolent of corporal smells;
but dreams will be reborn
to chase away the ghosts and demons
that frighten the children of our loins
in this land our land
this people, our people.

For Tenu and Afetsi

A Hymn

A crane carried my children
little bright eyed Afetsi, the last tree in the fence,
his brother Tenu, the homestead
is now steady-
inconsolable comrades;
we romped in Brazil once
now only a place of our blood binding imaginings.

Then we heard the generals
and the politicians, leaders
and elders of state
flagmen and ingenous braggarts
scream obscenities on street corners
as winds whirlwinds rose
storms abating

in miraculous hours
of a night remembered
when the children slept
as I cradled them in little balls
till the dying moments
of a fury and a tempest;
of leaders, generals, and headmen
once promissory agents of fates
postponed in the hills
along shorelines denuded
houses gone where
the sea eats the land at home
still eats the whole land at home.

Corn as agent
in libatory offerings here, blood, yes
always some blood
part of the covenant with corn and gods
exploring that noon the battlefield
certain that original victories
will be renewed here
in the glowing dusks
and obsolete dawns refurnished
for wars that must be fought
anew and anew again;
blood, yes always some blood,
trickles in menstrual measures
watering births born afore
the kid's mantlers readied
for an outdooring sanguine serious
hurting, but calm,
like the after fury of the sea
that still eats the land at home.

In Havana, now my love city
steeled and tempered in the Fidelista fire,
I raise a voice across time
oceans and chains
against the slave days of my life,
ancestral hurts I hurl them back
at all the organizers of my fate,
I reject once more the silence of the manacle
the cooing of the dawn doves
and the bluejays of my Kalamazoo days;
I rejoice in you the girl of freedom
you whom I sang in asphalt cities
and prison yards, you
the refrain I hummed in our forgotten villages

I come again to Havana
23 years to the day
cocky brassy city
where victorious armies hang their banners.

I continue my song, noon song
left unfinished in 66
a half-finished meal
abandoned to sand and wind;
songs are builders' dreams, you said,
architectonic symphonies of joy
or hate or love
irremedial as abortive efforts
at goodness or grace
left intact in some Sahelian pauper's field
not enough to appease
this millennium old hunger of my people.

Anyidoho in song raised the truth;

we have people,
we too have people.

By what margin of doubt
shall I measure this pain
ineffable historical immense?
Herding freedom children into playing fields
under gun nests manned by dogs of war?

I came again to my dream city
Havana, not for the architecture
Spanish American to the core
but to recall my gladiatorial days
in imperial cities
where once I marched
in the ranks of Caesar's armies
I was the dark sword bearer
abandoned in upper Gaul;
centuries later my ancestral shield
was resurrected to adorn
the cathedral at Yamousoukro.

And Frenchmen, though dead
shall tell the fate of Africa-
endorse the name of la Côte d'Ivoire
sublimated by phallic christian temples
against measurements given and demanded
by those whose gunmen
killed us in Lusaka, Memphis, Soweto, and Harare.

They come again feasters on negro fetuses
their bloody banners proclaiming
"structural adjustment, rescheduling of debt"
aid recycled even in the body

of the green monkeys of our homeland
—acquired immunity deficiency—
the syndrome completes the symmetry
of hunger and death

Then they proclaimed human rights
and democracy, yes the rights
of all to die of their chosen ailments,
of hunger in a world richfull
of grain arms beef chemicals and milk.

I wanted to rise and go to Santiago
to see the long nosed S.O.B.,
who killed Allende
in the name of the American Liberty
and barricaded that freedom city
sung of in moving cantos by Neruda.

What sin is this that endures
slave ships whips chain gangs
and jeering nigger insults forever
in subhuman cities
where we inhabit crumbling tenements
and wear their cast-offs at home
and abroad?
—acquired immunity deficiency syndrome—
the ailment imposed by greed
and death and
green monkeys, innocent
as the dawn that lifted in the Olduvai,
companions in this valley of wills and hope—
of struggle and victory
of victory and struggle
against the equinoctial hate

dark plots and stratagems of power
to win over death and dying.
Keep the faith, my boys
after I am gone.

Of Niggerhood

Memory told me I'd been here before
once upon an age
now lost in ocean water
companioned by flying fish
across a briefer ocean
a much briefer ocean

I this man graying
won little victories
in little inconsequential wars
absorbed immemorial moments
or else forsaken saying
for a leafy plain and open country
beside a little river
running home in my sea.
Give me a place of peace and love along vertical hills
symmetrical with my enduring will,
please give me still to dream and dare;

I lift a fist
in greeting
Love alone conquers all, some fool said,
I wish it were true
I truly wish it were true.

A Death Foretold

Sometimes, the pain and the sorrow return
particularly at night.
I will grieve again and again tomorrow
for the memory of a death foretold.
I grieve again tomorrow
cull a flower across the yard
listen to the birds in the tree.

I grieve again tomorrow
for a pain that grows on
a pain a friend of my solitude
in a bed long emptied by choice;
I grieve again this grievance
immemorial for
     this pain
this load under which I writhe and grieve.

Yesterday I could not go
for my obligatory walk,
instead I used the hour
to recall the lanes, the trees
the birds, the occasional snarling dog
the brown sheep in a penned field
the dwarf mango tree heavy with fruit
the martian palms tall and erect
the sentry-pines swaying
in a distant field.

I believe in the possibility of freedom
in the coming of the bees in summer
in mild winters and furious hurricanes;

I believe in the arrival of American tornadoes
before I go to hunt
on the island of youth
where I smelt the heady smell
of the wild guinea fowl
and heard her chuckle for her child
in the opening light of an April day.

I believe in hope and the future
of hope, in victory before death
collective, inexorable, obligatory;
in the enduring prospect of love
though the bed is empty,
in the child's happiness
though the meal is meagre.
I believe in light and day
beyond the tomb far from the solitude
of the womb, and the mystical night,
in the coming of fruits
the striped salmon and the crooked crab;
I believe in men and the gods
in the spirit and the substance,
in death and the reawakening
in the promised festival and denial
in our heroes and the nation
in the wisdom of the people
the certainty of victory
the validity of struggle.

Beyond the fields and the shout
of the youth, beyond the pine trees
and the gnarled mangoes
redolent of childhood and prenativity,
I am affronted by a vision

apparitional, scaly
lumbering over a wall
raising a colossal bellow.
His name is struggle.
He is my comrade and my brother
intimate, hurt, urgent
and enduring.

I will not grieve again tomorrow.
I will not grieve again.

The Prophecy from Iran

And the speaker from Iran said to the Philistines of Gaza,
behold, rise and seize the aeroplanes and ships, bomb the
shops of the Christians of the West so that they heed your
plight and prevail upon the Israelites to let your people
go. And the leaders of the Christians of the West in one
great and agonized voice screamed saying ho, ho, ho see how
evil they are, these bad men of Qom and Teheran who in their
iniquity incite vile cruelty against Christians and
peaceful men. Alas and behold the Christians of the West
heard not the cries and the weeping of the children of the
Philistines in Gaza; they heard not the mourning cries of the
dying women and children crushed against the ancient walls of
Jerusalem; oh, they heard not the dying whimper of Allah's
children in the camp of Sabra and Shatillah when the
Christians under the orders of the Israelites, once children
of God, put men to the torch and the fire. They heard not the
dying cries of the perishing souls of Gaza. And the Lord's
heart was full of sorrow for the children of Israel

whom he delivered once from captivity
and returned to the land he promised them, for they commit
evil against his children. And His heart was also full of
compassion for the children of the Philistines whose land He
gave to the children of Israel.
And it was the first day on the new dawn of creation in the
year of our Lord nineteen hundred and eighty-nine in the
beautiful month of May when the grass was green and birdsong
was heard in the land of Tyre and Sidon, in Jerusalem and
Gaza, in Lebanon and Damascus—all under the cross the
crescent moon and the six-pointed star of David.

In Memoriam

Return to Kingston

For Neville Dawes (1926–1984)

Again, we come again to Kingston
to bury Neville, nay cremate
him who fell in Mandeville
victim of neglect carelessness and rum
consign him to the original fire
    that nurtured him.

Memory, Memory,
    you have held the door ajar
these years;
on that day in the cathedral
as we wept on the bier of a brother
ashen, peaceful, silent;

gone like the furious wind of the hurricane month
that gave him to the fire that nourished him.

I met him, an old African
in a village somewhere in Middlesex
sweeping and carting off autumn leaves.

Through all these changing places
I saw my people:

in the slums and cold tenements
on the urine-wet floors of tram-ways
in fields long harvested by their owners
in sad subliminal houses with Jericho's walls
their ancient warrior gait now shuffles
across uneven grounds;
they used to sing once
songs of the native land
of absence
        of family and clan
of heroes who went empty-handed to war;
they sang of nuptial nights
of moons swaying beyond palm trees
of evening fires lit with flimsy twigs
for the gathering warmth of the tale time;
they sang, these men in rags now,
of kings, rulers and true democrats,
of miracle-men who transformed cobras into twine,
of un-believers and God fearers,
embracing hope and the sharing harvest of hope.
I see them now limp across snowfields
fired on storm nights
of blazing friendless territories of exile
and exile tears;

Recall again oh gods, the fire in my stomach
the same fire we consigned them to
centuries ago in Kingston, Alabama, and Port au Prince.

They will come to share with me
the lean bread and the fragile hope of Havana,
the handful of shrimps smoked on slow fires,
the garnished snapper in full green and red,
the lingering faith in a bountiful future.

Neville, brother, I came back.

I met only Maxwell who mentioned your name
and looked sadder than I have ever known him
I came back to your native city
walked in fear of the crouching lions of your blue mountains
shivering of a malignant fever in the barnyard of a slave city
my ancestral woes intact from Africa
etched upon a hill here
my slavery days of collective dance
when we sang in chains of home
across the sea and the equinoctial hour.

I saw them on the edge of Spanish Town
where Mr. Thomas clutched his ancient pipe
and spat upon the retreating mulatto girl
with the high behind.
King Cudjoe went into the hills
and concluded a disastrous treaty with the enemy.

On Hagley Park I saw my brother
matted hair ruined eyes and yet
a booming voice denouncing the iniquities
of Babylon whilst the distant sea

my mirror and the narrow world my tomb
boom across a bay where the caravels are drowned
that brought me here.

I come again I say
half-clansman of the ritual goat
tethered to a forgotten tree
in a ruined and alien field;
I am the last dancer in the circular team
kicking only dust
after the graceful ones are done,
the jeers and sneers echoing
down the vast saharas of my history
on whose corner
this day, this natal day,
I weep anew
for historical follies I could not shed
abilities I did not realize
victories I did not savor
hopes I did not endure

I salute very warmly, all comrades
far and near,
some who shared dreams with me
and died in foreign lands
some who jumped ship to join the winning sides
in London, Paris, and San Francisco
where I once passed
to check my diminishing account
and order the latest models in books

Toasts we drank return
to remind me of serious moments,
of commitments that will not wait

to struggle with the people.
The meals we shared
at early sunset or sunrise
in smoke-filled rooms redolent with conspiracy
and strategies; the whispers we exchanged
the notes we wrote on details of action
and ideological certitudes
revision—of slogans and tactical maneuvers;
the flags we designed in silence and secrecy
for malformed and non-existent brigades
marching as to war
determined columns shorn of hope
and cheer; we led a throng
into the same groves of childhood
steered we were on the flat wood
steadied by a single simple choice
renewing we did ancestral oaths
that when our palm trees prosper
we surely cannot die of thirst.

Under the trees, under the trees
and the rain will come and beat me.
I sang that diviner song
long ago at home in levity and jest
again in passion and faith
on podiums and hills,
in the natal village of Asiyo.
I sang that song in the paternal home
sea-front smashed by the sea
demolishing remnants of the German church
original from Bremen in wood
against the Christian hymn
"he whom the Lord loves
He sends farthest afield."

We sang these songs before
in the endless seasons of fish
blue-claw and the grinning oyster
the fat horse-makerel and flat-sole
together with the howling salt-water sprat
and the dome-shelled crab loaded
with unforgettable oils—
all, companions of the roasted corn-meal
soaked in the arrogant gusto
of the original fat of the king palm.

We carried our songs into the Easter cities
paschal as our original sin,
into port- towns and open roads,
village lanes, cooper's sheds
and smithy shops where we shod the horse
for the journey at dawn;
we sang before the sauce sizzled
and raged in the morning of the meal day
before the arrival of the christians and the masters.

Then I smelt the rum shops and the cooking
heard a hymn feminine and ardent
"Make a joyful noise unto the Lord"
and the doors of Babylon closed again,
this time behind me
with Neville and I on the freedom train,
going home, yes, going home.

Lover's Song

There was a time under a bridge
in a foreign country, if I recall,
she came shy weepy.
I told her of love
  and of love's sadness
  solitude and an empty bed.

She answered with silence
dropped a necklace into the grass
turned her head to watch a star.
Then she embraced me kindly
and left a pain in the grass.

The Red Bright Book of History

Blood on the Tianamen
verminous flags, an obscenity
of a naked whore bearing a torch
in the harbor of a wicked city;
drowned immeasurable blood
in Beijing

The scrolls are rolled back
we hear anew the trampling long march
Mao and his comrades bright-eyed from Yenan
the red army has indeed crossed the Tatu River
but not every face is smiling!

Gun nests manned by youth
squared against youth in Tianamen
in the place where demons once held sway
the spring wren found no nesting place

Tanks, artillery, the infantry is in town,
the blast of the penultimate hymn
"The East Is Red" heard
above the tramp of the funeral march.
Oh China, Tunghuo, what hyena entered the fold
of your lambs
and wrecked the millennium of dream

Tell me into what final purgatory
have they pushed your soul?
You once ate on dunghills, Tunghuo
Your beggars used to line the entrance
of the cavernous tombs of greed
        near the forbidden gates of the sealed city.

But a dawn bright and eloquent
Lifted on your brow in 49.
You chased away the querulous nights of pain.
But now Tunghuo, martial tramps
and rattling arms are heard
on Tianamen.

A gate of heavenly peace?
The East is indeed red
now the red army fears indeed the long march!
banners victorious banners
soaked in blood;

The long march is the tramp of death?

the victorious struggle is the death of faith?
and the permanent revolution a blaze of lies?
Tunghuo, Tunghuo, Tunghuo
the talons of the eagle have been paired
the heels of the brave have been broken
Mao weeps inconsolably
Among the ruins of Ting.
Tu Fu the original prophet
has moved his little boats
to the Potomac,
    and the Yangtze is mistaken
renamed alas for the Hudson.
Blood, Chinese blood flows
on the Tianamen in the lovely month of June
spring Beijin flowers blooming
on Tianamen square

June 1989

At a Time Like This

That a hut-place is not a shrine
thatched in seasonal days
with dry grass and palm
fronded generously by the maker,
nature's gift to the native earth
all the creatures in their space.

How the skies bleed
on a moon eclipse in 47
when David came home on a market day

in that town where father
kept shop and
made clothes for the village boys.

At a time like this,
I recall the wasted day
the frivolous hour
spent cutting my nails,
the singular melancholy
deaths of family and friends—
the gnawing shame
that I could have done more
for my fellowman and brother.

These hours now recalling the cruelty
the inconsonant ultimate hurt
administered by once-upon friends
grown arrogant with office and power.
We structured a dream, you and I
once along salt-flats at home,
dried river beds strewn
with skeletal remains
of shame and heroic intentions
conch shell-full
of noble gestures marooned
in dry beds our shame.

I will, I swear seek a hill
of infinite tribulations
and particular sins
where rivers of blood tributary flow
and dead men in bone are real
in valleys of crushed dreams
and remnants insects-gnats

smashing each little darkness
my kingdom, outrage,
my morality and little hours of courage
leaving intact my faith and honor,
my blood, my home,
     my name.

When these flimsy tinsels peel off
leaving denuded enamels of bones
stark as age to be disguised
disposable shells of some honorable men
shit-eating s.o.b.s and swindlers
purveyors of reversible truths
posing as guardians of the sacred word
and arguable morality,
these creepy flawed timbals
of cacophonous dismay!

I shared tears and sorrow once
in freedom's name, I say,
stood stoutly by friends and comrades,
defended a common turf of faith
     and nation
lost no honor
in the name of no compromise
raised a howl alongside
the victorious army
and wrote my name
in the Red Bright Book of History.

Back with Sandino

The park that harbors the volcano
was shut on the Monday, *lunes* that is;
the gateman enigmatic as his smile explained.
Five years ago the volcano
was deep sulfurous.
On the road from Managua to Masaya
occasional jams relieved
by young soldiers armed with a smile
inspecting car papers
waving us on with a smile unarmed.

Five years the open-eyed smile
condor, a limbless youth
led by a wet-eyed bride
across the road.
The lovers are fewer,
the green is sharper in the new park
against where we placed a flower
twice for Carlos Fonseca;
the wren song of the evening hour
is clearer, deeper
as the last battle steadies
for the final try.

Banner will wave again, comrades
here in Sandino's country
the cry of heroes dying
in volcanic hills,
children and coffee pickers dying
compesinos left only with dreams
of the flat tasteless tortillas

lean ribs caged in struggle
for this piece of the authentic America.

Give them liberty or
    oh, give them death.

On the road to Masaya
I saw the sign post to Grenada
where once in your company
I dreamt on a noon
the resurrection of an island
from a cemetery of dead atolls;
the clenching fist
of an island on the blue Atlantic edge
where Maurice died of treachery and greed
before the coming of the North Americans
under a reganite banner
soaked in inconsolable blood.

In Bluefields, a hurricane
came one night
flattened peasant homes and food fields
and hurried across the hills.
Charity, her hands over her head
wept in the ruined city all night
for bread and cover from the equivocal rain
Oh, she wept, and wept and wept;
the Christians and democrats,
human rights and amnesty agents
set their collective face
in perfect scorn!
Human rights, human rights!
human rights for those
who will be as we whose

charity is the miracle of the donor's faith
Hurrah! Cesaire said,
hurrah for those, who invented nothing!
I, Awoonor, forded rivers
crossed paths on daunting hills
seeking that Kingdom
promised by my father.
I pawned all my childhood gifts, toys
and certainties for an infinity
of grace and creature comforts
inane hours loaded with fear and loathing
for a fake and living God
hypocritical as a loudly threatening rain
and gaping cannons on the forts
that will either fire or fall.

Managua, June 1989

Prayer

My hands clasped now as always, my fathers;
I spent counting hours
commemorating this line running
from far away tortuous pillars
in a mudhouse somewhere, somewhere
down that edge of chains and pains
where the birth chamber
in my grandfather's house far away
in Asiyo
Give me patience to last
this penultimate treachery, masters.

I count with you the beads
to the solemn koranic reading
Bissimillahi! Allah Akbar!
permit us gray ones,
to chew through this nut
cracked yet wholed in seeds
ready for the new breeds of my stalwart loins

Teacher, repeat the prayer over my head
repeat that prayer, teacher,
summon again the old man you sent me
remnant my ancestral head
who walks all lanes
flies all skies
fords all rivers with me
buoyed by my original bow
rain-bent by my serpents of Whyddah
in intimate embrace
of that earth that nursed us together.
Ancient one, rest now with me
in alien beds in friendless cities
calm with insomniac nights
with your cool hands and voice;
send me messages of hope and victory
for the time that will surely come.

I saw him last dawn
this ancestral brother and comrade
trailing remnants of my umbilical cord
carrying the last bits of my circumcision
scouring the intimate earth
looking again for my oath
and promise,

Again I saw him last night
young as the sun in the morning
blazing shy half musing smile
eyes shut averted, only briefly.

After a little coaxing
he raised up his head
stared into my dreaming soul
awakened once more in me
the tangible embers of the spirit
and the promise.

The Ancient Twine

Certain hours, I, enslaved
by intangible thoughts translated
as love vibes into precise mysteries
and miracles, succumb to an occasional joy.

I came in my time home
avoiding singular and unique disgraces
embracing skeletal whores and
declaring them stunning beauties.
I smile once at the original folly.

The merciful rain on the verge
of consoling May winds
harbingers of the season of hurricane
and burning fields of cane

I chose a time clear and clean

inimical and lovable
to assess the ultimate caress
and those steady moments
terminal points in a lifesong
sung at home sweet
and low among alien people

loud together
in a fabric loomed with an ancient twine
threaded here resilient
toughened by mixes of herbs wine and blood.

"Raise the song for me, my Kinsmen
I am gone, I am gone. There is nothing more to be
said."

Seatime, Another

(for A.E)

So I rode
a safer ship
sail-turned tug-rolled
in seas long known of alien coasts
to this apparent safe haven.

Who can tell where any bird will fall?

We took you to that island
on the tip of marble hills
with remnant ancient palms and pines
green against our Atlantic.

You were distraught, I saw,
yet expectant of a time of returns
and hope, hesitant yet certain
that the flight of the eagle
shall precede the nesting time.
We will organize our meager meals
after production days
when we can count every ear of corn.

I recall clearly the cockcalls
of early dawn in that alien city.

What consoling I need do
I shall do before tears mature
I shall do before tears are let fall.

What consoling I need do
I will do before death,
that intrepid harvester of fields he didn't plant,
comes calling
with his own distinct bouquet of flowers.

What consoling of the people we need do,
let us do it now
as our road will surely end
in the man's inordinate field.

Readings and Musings

I was reading again this morning,
on the loo the poet who jumped over a bridge;
I remember the golden legged girl called
oh her name I forget;
but I cannot forget the sunset yesterday.
At the Marina Hemingway
I played a demon game
recalled a miraculous place Stony Brook
on that island where I left
all my friends and lovers

Yesterday I quarreled with this girl
not quarrel, well just an argument, mind you
when she thought we will not be good enough
at midnight
and early dawn when I drove her home
to the East of the city
past the abandoned lovers at the sea-wall
locked in perpetual embrace
passed blue-clad policemen
marooned in articulate conical boxes
on the corner of every *calle* or *avenida*
I returned home as the new sun was rising
to seek the certitude of my bed
with my self-esteem intact
and my honor inviolate

Light Hours in Verse

evening settles,
    slow deliberate
over strains from a Ravel symphony,
melancholy, sad, saccharine if you say;
I prop up the second pillow, gently
and recalled a loved one very far away
I read a sign across the ugly wooden frame
full of goblinic images with gnomic tendencies
for a revelation, a premonition
of a road left to be walked.
I have trod gently too many
already, too too many,
taken too many careful steps
Counted too may cautionary winds
read too many threatening letters
walked away from too many fights
and dared too few turbulent storm.

I glean in a supreme prophecy
the tight possibility of a journey
a new course on another road
in another country
where they know my name
so infinitude, light, sad
violinic harmony of a perfect life
(to be followed by a perfect death
long foretold)
sometimes full of love and laughter
intimate hours of enormous joy.

What particular patterns are revealed here

against a crushing blue sky
in worlds threatened by rains
which we feared once
alongside booming cannons
on a prison wall and yard at home
which we no longer fear?

Where a donkey once broke a fence
brayed in the yard awhile
fled across the fields
and was seen no more;

the brief notice said
Sergei Alexandrovich Yesenin
the poet of the revolution
knotted a cord, recorded roses
and took his life in 25
to an ungodly hereafter
12 years later, General Konstantin Konstantinovich Rokossovky
    was released and reinstated to his military rank,
    —minus his teeth—

Ravelian strains record again
an intimate sorrow and invisible tears.
I will weep no more against the wind
I shall cry no more in the rain.

Time Revisited

Time will wipe us out
inevitably as it does the April bee
or the welling surf of the ceaseless sea;
but there is a renewal point
as precious as the new skin on the cobra
transforming an uncertainty
into the precise shape of the new bud
of the coming corn.

Songbirds I knew as a boy
resing those matutinal hymns
dirge and praise once heard so long
oh, so long ago again
in the red earthed village
in the tree-lined ubiquitous country.

A Thin Echo of Time's Voice

With what can I seal the wound
cover the sores
that gnaw till the marrows
and the heart string
taut and tender unto pain.
Oh, these aches of all absence
memory of the trees at the birth-place
the earth-space ancestral as the name
emptied steadily of those stalwarts
who go, one by one, into the eternal oblivion,

blood-bound heroic singular men
and the women nubile
with tremulous voices
that raised all our dirges at death hour
merciful as God's grace
unto death.

There was the story of the people of the sun
who came one noon harvest time
to steal farm produce;
a farmer surprised them
cut the ropes
and marooned them on earth.

They are still here
Light and red as the earth
the men from the sun.

I remember him well, my last grandfather,
Deku, tall sinewy
spent all his life in the coffee fields
came home with his simple clothes to die;
he went home to his fathers at 90
if anyone can count the years.

There was a thin echo of time's voice
I recall, distinct, fearful
sailing on a wind
caressed by family love and original poetry.
(by family I mean more than husband and wife
    more than three or five)

We shall rise again, I say
we the children of Awoonor and Ashiaghor's houses

heroic defiant glorious
like clenched fists
solemnity was a drug we took
once in sorrow's house
when death made war upon our home
and termites ate the trees in the fence,
that was an age of tears and memorials,
of burials at dawn before the noon sun;
that was the time of recording and recall,
of history and family affairs
redeemed and returned to ancestral homes
only to be scattered once more to despair's winds.

There were some who resurrected the name
the owner of clothes
and installed heirlooms
gave up thundergods found on the high seas
found a dynasty that still reigns across imperial
boundaries.

We know where our arms were stored
where our feet were shod
where our birds and rivers
were kept intact by consoling winds

I, bearer of our heritage
found a crown on a dunghill,
am saddled now with the task
of wearing this sad lonely crown
of hope.

"As Long as There Are Tears and Suffering, So Long Our Work Will Not Be Over," Jawaharlal Nehru

Indeed, looming once again,
tentative, miraculous, and certain,
that surging will to march on
against odds and odds
against the prejudicial smirks and sneers
record again the task fulfilled
hoist a banner for the waging battle
march in the ranks of our people,
our black African people, footstools and heroes,
lynched, massacred, chained in alien lands
whipped under almond trees, trifled with, abused,

as long as there are tears and suffering,
our work cannot be over.

The Girl that Died in Havana

I cannot now recall where the cemetery is
being a stranger here. We bore her
on a lofty truck loaded with flowers
she was 19 and weighed very little
Round face, velvet skin, black jet eyes
well, they were closed when I saw her
This little girl my first assignment.

We passed through the door
jammed with soldiers, uniformed, without arms
They had also come for a comrade.
Did he die in a foreign war,
or did he perish in his own bed?
We passed through a long solemn hall
She lay in state, the girl.
Her friends were seated as at home.
One or two wept silently.
There was her friend from Ethiopia
restless and fretful as a mother hen
whose only chick a hawk had snatched.

Someone started a Christian hymn in our tongue
about a Kingdom far away
where there is no suffering
and evening shadows never fall.
The hymn stuttered and collapsed.

We sat stony faced and looked on.
Death the harvester has cut another green fruit yet
in a garden he did not plant.

The time came for us to go
to take her to the burial ground in the strange city;
our convoy, unusually long for this city
where death is no mystery or stranger
and the state orders it neatly
    and efficiently.

We missed the hysteria, the tears
the drinking and the swearing
the serious messages for the gone-befores
here death is a familiar neighbor,
the removal man who clears heroes' fields.

In the cemetery, the handlers
were happy agile around the light body.
She weighed very little
this little girl from Africa
that died in a distant friendly land.

They lowered her gently if a trifle carelessly.
We offered one prayer,
someone poured libation to the ancestors in our tongue.
The grave was a deep concrete cavern.
One or two shed a tear
We left her in the concrete garden
and went away, the little girl
who died in the strange city.

       my first assignment.

Our Pride Alone

I will indeed record
all pains, all joy
I will indeed record
all hurts, all shames.

Then in that penultimate hour
when our pride alone
is not enough
and the edge is close,
and our glorious family name
does not hold even
as it harbors remnants
of slavery, slaver ancestors and wealth

even as it shields hardy peasants
warrior sojourners from old tyrannies.

Some fool recalls a falling star
and the girl he kissed in a bar
in a far country, 28 years ago
of an early summer, returning from Moscow
en route to Paris with Neville, London,
all cities of conquerors, bright
lingering daylights and somnolent nights.

We broke the wings of a duck
alive after the hunt.
Days after it flew away
as my son played with it.

So seals dance in the arctic seas,
dolphins, ancestral as the monkeys
flap about leading us to safe havens
in our tropical oceans.

Resurrect that dream,
the search for the body of the man
I killed, the girl I lost;
suns do dance on the palm leaves
even in the rain; I heard
a tart laugh
on a night, hypnotic as a drug
and I was strengthened.

Dream—Again

For E. B.

She arrived, the dream of a distant home
    and time, shy nubile
precise bird-like gestures
perfect as our morning sun.

Why, someone asked is this thing
so good, generous, oh so good
at this time of age?

Memory, I answered; anxiety perhaps,
the need to reconstruct what is missed
over distant hills, seas, and time,
eternalize a sunrise and a happy morning
between erection
    and resurrection
of once a time upon a special land
by a unique river quietly flowing home
record the smell of the meal
the aroma of that girl
that tang of that wine
the rustle of that little wind
in that absent tree.
Perhaps it's to recall the memory
of a birth, yours,
on the bare earth of grandfather's house
at Asiyo.

So love this thing blooms again
saying with someone
that when I die
You this thing shall never die.

New Rain

Soon, the sundrenched fields
roar, resonant flowers aglow
made live by the putrescence
of a corpse planted
by a few years ago village skirmish
wherein all victims were forgotten
by retreating enemies.

The clatter of new rain
scatters a few searchers for boundaries
still reeking with the fact of death
on a bright day of a week in hell,
or heaven,
as we record a missal
of a childhood once upon a place
when God was white, bearded
      and inexorable.

Do we really like those things
we love, deny those plausible remnants
of pure happiness
      a drinking carousing
      and kissing time
lavish with sorrow
and memory's pains?

How does the worm's kingdom
resemble our particular constructions
of dream houses as sea and river fronts,
besides a lazy water flowing away
      and away?

I embrace each lover anew
of all my days
suspend each hour
of hate, proclaim a reprieve
for a consoling purgatory
a limbo where they say bodies
    are cleansed
hoist the simple fact aloft
that this instance is worthy
needed of record and celebration;
this love is good as the drink
after the rain, incontrovertible nourisher
feeder of our earth for grain
beans meat of the billy goat
for a festival renewal and beginning
for sheer indestructible joy.

Birds on an Autumn Wire

Turning suddenly I saw
the two birds brown green
flit off the wire
swift against a flashing wind
that whipped the silent trees.

I turned away from the rejection
when I looked again
    there stood on the wire
    a solitary bird.
The wind had stopped.

Then I looked again
the wind was still.
I saw five trees
the first half-perched
the last green-black erect
emerging distant from a bank of clouds
defiant as a hill
    on a yielding plain.

The birds came again
    chatty quarrelsome
garrulous against the silent
    watching world.

Then I saw the house for the first time,
a bay window, a grill
an antenna to catch
a sound or a vision?
The keen eye projects a miracle;
the sombre calm world remains
the one eternity
    long teared with sorrow
    long furrowed by the ploughman.

Shamla Hills

Bhopal

It was not that I forgot
or let slip into frivolous substitutes
or daily chores, that I forgot,
nor was it a simple act of neglect
that singular capacity we develop
sure of a place in crowded history
of our ultimate morality
of age and inevitable deterioration
of arteries, bones, of tissues and blood;
it could not have been that I forgot
the grim harvest of greed on a slope
somewhere, somewhere, Bhophal,
to be precise, Luanda, Maputo,
Njamena, and the many debris cities
Soweto, Mamalondi, Alexandra, all
erected by the masters of historical greed.

On Shamla Hills, I saw a sunset once
with Ernesto, César, and Okara
rosette, brilliant
illuminating its own eternal certainty
that the work of MAN AND GOD is not done!

It cannot be that I have forgot

Shamla Hills

Sanchi Temples

The Hindustani Latex Ltd. of Trivandrum
placed this advert in the Poetry Festival Journal
Bhopal, January 11–17,

> "For the first time in India
> world's thinnest condoms
> MOODS
> skin-thin luxury condoms
> Nothing else comes close enough."

Gossamer thin angel edge
light like ancestral meals
ritual light,
for how long will they preach
that all India needs
is a gigantic condom?

Somewhere in this vast arena
tragic as sea and air disasters
shipwrecks quakes and deep rivers
cancelled by man-made fate
structured by greed in boardrooms
multi-national as the wood's journey
around a table at which sat God's rivals
ingenious intellects our apocalypse.

On Shamla Hills, we breathed air
sulphur clean, sharp paschal avenging
the monks saffron-clad shorn

teeth yellowed by betel
original as the deities in the hills
abandoned among chattering monkeys.
That day, on the road to Sanchi
past chemical plants, hovels
bazaars, we edged a road
narrow as the goodness path
sharp, cross, tiringly patrolled
by bored overseers loaded
with discarded overcoats
of some reject mill.

Sanchi, breath-taking valley town
overlooking half-way a stunning plain.
Surely, armies have clashed here,
Mongol, Tartar, foreign warlords expeditionary
forces of some empire
here on the way to a victory
or carnage and death
in a valley green and ripe
with fruit and meat.

From the temples we stood
aghast not at the folly or the grandeur
at man's vision of God,
intricate obscene patterns of his majesty
divinely linked
        on this eternal hill
        of man's desiring.

It was God himself
inevitable as the rising sun
who astounds with his striving
on that plain below

his dwelling place once
now at rest in peaceful fields
his meagre and sufficient gifts intact
for his little brown children
on this precious real estate.

Childhood

When a boy, I used to wander off
away from friends and games,
to seek a quiet place in the grass
or under the tree
to ponder in my child's head
the mystery of my being
of the ancestral thunder house of Sofe.

There was a more fearsome house at Gbota
whose dancers came with me to all by dreams,
as I leapt away
        to favorite haunts
squirrel groves protected always
by that uncle who sneaked off
by his own hand.

Where do we go when the world ends?
Where do we go? If we go
do we go with all our people?
To what hills or caves or fields
To what banks or sea-shores?
For each day that dies

over unfamiliar cities
rebuild my birthplace, my fathers . . .

Parting

so sound a note
of a tear dropped at a place
of wailing,
    confirm the prickle point
of thistles, brambles
    the sharp ritual edge
of pain, at parting.

Is that what it means
when we too,
    having soiled our little spot
    loved our lovers
    eaten the last meagre meal
    of seasonal fruits sweet-sour
    in a temporal place
    under our gods, overseen
    by guardian ancestors,
move on to another land?

You will come again perhaps
when I am more ready
when the season is calmer
and the hurricanes avoid our house
and the lights burn more bright.
You will come again my love,
Hasta luego then

From *Until the Morning After* | 1987

Life's Tears

Death's brother, poverty
is life's tears; so please hold it gently.
Firebrand in the farm
do not laugh when you hear the wailing afar
call the Yokoes
call them for me
so they listen to these matters
sorrow children do not die in sorrow.
Death, you the flagbearer on life's sea
the oarsman who ails not
lest the boat perish, I salute you.
I salute you again.
Where did crocodiles go
when fire hit the village?
Where did the crocodile's children go?
We sing sorrow songs in tears' valley
we have the promise
and the hope
that our palms shall prosper
so we shall never thirst,
hold it, hold it for another one
that we all hold it.
We have a savior.

So the World Changes

Where are they?
Awlesi's mother's trade collapsed
the children cried and cried
"call her for me, please call her for me"

The day the desert tree blossoms
is the feasting day for the fowls of the air
The evil fowls and the good fowls
The owner of the earth covers them in his cloth
promised them
when he holds the promise
Thirst shall not kill them
so the world changes
rain comes after the drought
the yam festival after the sowing time.
Do not lose heart,
have arms, we have shields
When the powder house falls
the mother fails to make war.
Some rivers there are you cannot swim
some strong rivers there are you cannot ford.

Life's Winds

A palm shield in the river bend
bend my life to life's winds
and fate
For love destroys and builds
its own citadels
ending always the miracle
in seeding time.
Along a hope hill and fields
when dreams crush like petals
in a protective foil
against our fate.
We move on, carrying I say
a singular faith in death
the only companion in this valley

An eagle flight flares in the open field;
field squirrels cover their hide
in covets of browny bush;
duck watered ponds with
wild lilies affirm a day
of good hunt and food.

Grains and Tears

The river rock has long resigned
itself to cold;
where did the female crocodiles go
when fire hit the village?
Where did they go
when fire reduced the houses to stump walls?

A grain grown in tears fields
for orphans not satisfied
implored to wash their hands,
is meal of life

Go and tell them I paid the price
I stood by the truth
I fought anger and hatred
on behalf of the people.
I ate their meager meals in the barracks
shared their footsteps and tears
in freedom's name
I promised once in a slave house in Ussher
to postpone dying until
the morning after freedom.
I promise.

Had Death Not Had Me in Tears

Had death not had me in tears
I would have seen the barges
on life's stream sail.
I would have heard sorrow songs
in groves where the road was lost
long
where men foot prints mix with other men foot prints
By the road I wait
"death is better, death is better"
came the song
I am by the roadside
looking for the road
death is better, death is much better
Had death not had me in tears
I would have seen the barges
I would have found the road
and heard the sorrow songs.
The land wreathes in rhythm
with your soul, caressed by history
and cruel geography
landscape ineffable yet screaming
eloquent resonant like the drums
of after harvests.
We pile rocks on terracing love
Carry the pithy cloth
to cover the hearths of our mother.

Come now, you lucky ones
come to the festival of corn and lamb
to the finest feast of this land
come, now,

your lovers have unfurled
their cloths
their thighs glistening like golden knives
ready for the plunging,
for the plentiful loving time.
To whom shall I turn
to what shall I tell my woes?
My kinsmen, the desert tree
denied us sustenance
long before the drought.
To whom shall I turn
to whom shall I tell my woes?
Some say tell the mother goat
she too is my kinswoman
elemental sister of your clan
But I cannot tell the mother goat
for she is not here.

Act of Faith

Where trees die deserts bloom
absence of water is thirst's companion
so we smash all grain for rain
cropping time for growth now
now when dying itself
is the ultimate act of faith

at home, the destined rulers
goaded the young men unto death
these hypocritical tax dodgers
and their fraudulent briefs and lies,

these leeches who live on the fat
of a lean country
devourers of corpses in fetal state
whose claim is supported by an ecclesiastical order
grown fat with ill-gotten gains,
receivers of stolen goods
these lawyers!
these professional acrobats!

I Rejoice

At departure time the family came
my mother silent as ever
my sister organized like an avenging army
her husband is a petty gambler and thief
the wives and their hypocritical relays
telling their woes and the misconduct of their children
and my father, I think I see my father
dead now these six years.
I've still to plaster the grave and
erect a marble head
and work out an inscription my sister says
with fitting quotes from the holy book
"Lord in Thy Gracious Keeping
Leave we now thy servant sleeping"
or words to that effect.
I know he sleeps not
torments my fitful sleep of midage
promises a fruitful turn in his failed field.

sparrows abound in our town

brown dunghill birds chirpers
unafraid of funeral gatherings and the
coming rain.

The Picture

At first a mound
a breast topped by a familiar
black nipple
edging itself with a vague sky
circled by little hills
milking itself no milk
but blood
always blood
Beyond, a far suggestion of a mountain
before a line of nims and bougainvillea
red in blooming time
It could be spring, but ours
is anytime of Year
rain or shine, anytime
when fate itself abounds
with nipple
reaches up heavenwards
looking for suckling mouths
and yellow moths.
Ours is anytime, a
anytime of Year.
So I promised a festival
that never came.
I shall redeem our ancient pledge.
I promise. I promise.

For Ezeki

As a plea on time's best conduct
I salute the homestead and the ancestors.

Someone told the lies
that buzzards feed on black carcass only.

After feasts in graves-end
where grains pile for homestead construction
we await the festival of hope
under the single lemon tree
flowering on the outskirts of ruined cities.

So you went home Zeke
to seek memories along the goat paths, home
to those lingering shrubs of childhood
denuded by exile tears.

We say
the snake that dies on the tree
returns home to the earth.

Again after many an absence
listen to the tramp and footfalls,
the thuddering fall of your body
hitting your earth anew.

And Zeke,
Tell them the youth
of the eagle dreams of years;
of the hope that burnt
in flames of incendiated cities;

of the time for meals and laughter
at night.
Of burial grounds and death
on bright afternoons of the equinox.

Tell them Zeke of the other storm lands
the crammed tenements
and burning snow fields;
of negros dying in Memphis
the same death once enacted in Ullundi

Tell them of the young men
that nod on the corners of national grandeur; tell them
of tears
abundant tears.

Tell them of Zambia and the burning trees,
of Accra, Nairobi,
of the pillars of salt
melting in Paris for the backward glance;
of Kampala of ribboned poinsettias
before the coming of Field Marshall Amin.

Above all Zeke
tell them of hope and the promise of hope
encrusted beneath death
and death's tears.
of the excellence
and the vision
that no perfect armaments can destroy;
of the human will that shall endure,
of the coming festival of corn and lamb
of the freedom day that shall rise
as the sun tomorrow.

Tell them also of the brothers up north
in the riverine and savannah fields
battling the hurricanes of hunger and the torments
of the inconsolable cactus.

Tell them too of those who went away
for seasons
but returned with ripening corn
and the tamed serpent.
Of those who did honor to the land
in the voluble chants then raised
of hope
and always of hope.

Of those who pointed to the native land
with their right fore finger
never with their left
and sang of the sea and the bluejays of Kalamazo,
and the streaked mackerel of Chesapeake Bay.

We sang of hills and plains, Zeke
you and I in those memorials
we forged in asphalt cities
locked in cold purgatories of absence and exile
"that we whom the gods love they send farthest afield."
Tread gently on the familiar earth
Tread very softly on your familiar land.
Let your cripple crawl I say
turn into a warrior's gait
But walk very softly on your ancestral earth.
for your victory
our victory.
Chinua, Mazisi, Okigbo, La Guma
Laye, Ngugi, Okot, Efua, Aidoo,

Brew, Okai, Rubadiri, and
I with your leave Zeke
add my name
For the coming excellence of days
For the lovely resurrection time.

Kofi Awoonor
Brasilia, Brazil
May 10, 1985

From *The House by the Sea* | 1978

Poems, Fall '73

Fall, sirens dulled by the grisly
smoke, exhalations, the divine order
suffers reversals and taut rope
dancers circling the citadel of cant
on this hardened earth miracle workers
in rented clothes search their hearts
for ancient amulets to effect
our resurrections

I shall pass through the eye
of the fornicating needle
my riches stacked
in a burlap bag
for the kingdom of heaven
seventy times seven
I'll help the dier die
gouging out the eyes of the Levites
and the money changers

My heart wounded my heart
in this still night of birth
and death
the removal man
reaper-angel of profaned destinies
locks the door and hides the keys

My love, the naked mirrors
of my soul, luminescent cancer
and the adoration
what profound mysteries there are
in the curvature of the rose

and the arc of the lonely autumn bee
doomed to die
as the earth dies.
On you I ground my pride
Fragmented clerks of the west
hurrying home at noon time
across lonely sonorous bays
where still rings the echoes of all
my days
I have wanted the friendship
of the manacle
and the luxurious joy of the rose.
My applications still pile high
till the day the voice is heard
for what splendour wrenched
for the victory time

My bird
held captive those centuries
was released this noon
into a void. Fluttering its wings
for lack of direction and basic hesitation
it flew into the glass windows

The Land Endures

patterned after blood-clots
insigniaed delivery's weeping body
flight to places where they lock the doors
            and hide the keys;
my father endures, so does my mother

miracle makers kingdom of life
in dawn's glories where the grain is citadel
      and prayer.
Dawn's glory; there is song
we shall sing it to the unison
of the blue heron
as the land endures again
     in our time

Going Somehow

for Richard and Barbara Priebe

There is not much to be said.
time has draped herself in mourning
wandering since last night over the hills
singing a dirge swallowing Afghans
in the night vomiting
the green streaks of my unrest

But somewhere somewhere they say
     tenderness endures.

We'll quieten our tears
on the asphalt underfeet
of the negro widows
who knew nothing of Pennsylvania
and the burning of the Jews
nor the miracle of Babi Yar
So the Russian frauds who knew nothing,
Brodsky with his deadly ignorance

Voznesensky and his motorcycle jacket
believing the world and its half-truths
       The flies buzz again in memory
         of him who fed the buzzards of Sharpeville
for whom there will be no Jewish appeal funds
nor congressional threats to cut off trade and traffic
and no Swiss villas and special coaches
    across the alps into the arms of
        our humanity.
    I'll dig the pit for you, someday.

For Pablo Neruda

Hombre, your passionate pleas
are understood, even the way you contrived
to die
escaping the shame of Ugarte and his cohorts
on the asphalts of Santiago.
Hombre of the lonely spots
your humanity was the banner you unfurled
long ago in the east among the cannonades
of the orient where heroes
long sung in the rubbered feet of Ho Chi Minh
and Mao on the long march,
Compadres planting the lamps in the east
raising litanies in the caves
and hope burnt in their eyes
in the trample of feet around those
inaccessible cathedrals.
You resurrected the myth of Lautaro
who ambushed the prey of eagles
wrenching liberty for the earth
and the earth
Even the vast sea of your cantos

could not encompass the boundaries
of your chant
as they salute the bandera of liberty
hallowing out of the very rocks
their forever secrets.

What is man, hombre, if he never
soiled his hands in the dirt of despair
if he never toiled in the meager
fields of the vultures compadres
who broke the law of the beehive
and erected the prison yards
by yardage and iron in the bosom of the earth?
Your legs were there hombre
when Ugarte with his cohorts
slit the throat of Salvador Allende
in the name of the American liberty
and you had to die.
Where are those liberating secrets
of Machu Picchu, tellurian man
and of the earth, your earth?
Where is *viejo corazon, olvidado*?

I await the secrets
I am part of you hombre
part of the octopus of this undying liberty

Requiem for Pablo

Where are those who swear,
poetry has nothing to do with it
"I don't want to be used for political causes"
they proclaim.
But the laugh is on them hombre.

As they carry their inanities in man hats
envenoming themselves like our early serpents
for a battle that will be fought
on this earth, our earth.

What seats do you occupy on which fathers'
right hand?
I cannot open the shrines now hombre
for night is here. But I will hide
and laugh in the weary triumph of your cause
I will see your shadow across the Santiago sky
With the company of your murdered compadres
composed with joy
spreading vigilant seedlings
to be born in the faeces of the hyenas
who too, in their own way
will and must fertilize our earth.
So ten times seventy times seventy
the full meter of your chant will be heard
in the crackling of the seed
in the swelling of the seed
and the dead shall rise
for your festival and your wake.

I heard your pleas in the night of my blood
those pallid temples rise in our sun
exuding the adamant stupidity of the
new warrior race
carving out conquered territories in deserts of despair
and memory stands by the temple gate
reciting the TORAH
clutching his nervous skull-cap
soiling his pants before the forced trip
into the ovens.

They can sing the obscenities of Jerusalem
as the sacrificial first fruits bleed
like the dying sun and the light
is out.

They cannot move in the manner of God
who fucks others people's wives
and leaves cash payment on the dresser
with a note promising
just promising
You, hombre, beheld the mercy tree
leafing in the wake of that autumn 1973
As God, oh God, his hair thinning
accompanies the marauding armies of Ugarte
shatters in his vulgar laugh of the cross
Your tears your tears
and I remember

Wole in the Nigerian jail
Okigbo in flight to the musical bust
the last dance of our drums.

I rememeber the anointment in dreams
the tyranny of his limb, your tomb too hombre
the denial of the accompanying bell
and the descant of flowers for the burial ground
We spent the cannibal hours
among hymns to dead comrades
amidst pyramids of tears
erected through our blood.
Pay them no heed, these desecrators
of already despoiled sepulchres.

You know I sang of the sea

my song I sang of the sea
in the plundering hours before exile
relieving me of the mortuary smells
then and now.

Some talk of lunar virgins
and magical feats in bloated jars
But I speak simply of home
and the goat on the cleft rocks
the lizards on the hills
the monkeys in the mountains

After the Exile and the Feasts

For Akosua

Over our heads in the blue night
streets darkening at scarcely afternoon
cold and the purgatory of allies and comrades
in the callousing hands of your care
survival and betrayal are one,
         as we are one;
while grace in the memory of our sons
and daughters will rule the land.
To master our grief
with fans of gassed birds
gasping with us long after
on the gothic beds of the American vulgarity.

Songs of sorrow repossess our hearts
memory itself lifted through these stunted trees

beyond Medina
under moons and tropical willows
not of mourning and tears

I gave you the seven suns of Anahuac
with the Mexican scents and leather goods
sombreros and guitars vomited by
the beggars in Nogales
for a quarter they sang blood
in the blue night of southern fogs

that noon our plane,
horizontal prophetic bird touched
down in Kalamazoo
where I didn't have a girl but you
for memory

and the joy of a new place I knew
once upon a sweltering summer
by bus past the lake
while Chicago rose with the blue haze
of its daily hate. I skirted
our sorrow gingerly like a soldier
missed by the last recovery patrol
crossing the mine
fields of my life
home to where the bugle calls
home to the drums
home to the hurrahs of
        defeat.

in your bosom I slept
placing my hands upon that firmament
where respite was long granted

and the curvature of your body's
amazing odor's amazing odor
like the howl of booted dogs fleeing
the pavement of our minds

because you cannot always perceive them except
in your own deep deep way I know
   we are safe.

Some Talk of Lunar Virgins

I heard today of a South African thug telling lies to school children in Bellport about our land. I wanted to march down and get hold of the scurvy fellow by the scruff of the neck; but there are laws here too, and instead I write you a poem.

Through this night of hurt and of stone
I heard the captive birds and the exile birds
singing once more in their dreams
while the bayonets of the executioners
lie idle upon the asphalts
naked, more naked
than the very waters of our soul.
Those who are guilty of incest
and suicide represent the equilibrium
of sanity, and like the madmen of my hometown
theirs is the glory and the honor.
I return my friends to the black lunacies
of our land, your land
I go to sculpt the passions of our despair
on my land's granite soul
with our own knives

that I may carve away this vertigo
which now torments the lyrical lineaments
of my heart.
All doors are my doors my friend
open now unto a gnawing
raw brutal day, the first
of our astronomic legend and fact
rolled around the marble coils
of their heart

Poem

let me touch you now
where it most hurts
in the corner of your heart
the little petals in my feet
will yield fruits
    in a season of rain
for a jubilee
let us call our comrades
home from the wars

Poetry

So I spoke of it, I claimed
I knew it long long ago
in the voluble boasts
of the cantors of my hometown

in the zenbuddhist cantata of Snyder
and the jazz and agony of Michael Harper
in the long elegies of Kunene
in the last last foot fall of our
launching armies
   against death,
     against death's tears
In the name of the corn
and the desert bread,
in the name of the magic
of drink and libation
for the lone fly dead
  in the wine

Departure and Prospect

Seven years, and I'd like
to care for the dying,
clean sores in the iodine mornings
on tropical grasslands and scapes;
I'd like finally
to start the foundations of my dream house
Smell again the pubic groin
of my ravished earth.
I'd like to talk to adjudicators
of my fate, insist on the issuance of a judgment.
I have, praise be to my ancestors,
I have sold my fear forever
for a mess of potage in the American wolf's lair
And I am not afraid.
I joined the crowd of the exodus, seven years

in the convex history of Africa, an egg
in my hand, pursued by the unutterable choir boy
who sang the dirge at our first funeral,
Death, the accordionist of the night
played the hymns my brothers couldn't hear,
wearing his own crown of rags
and putrescent armors
leading the carnival.
The children swore in tears
But I left, for no one could hear my cries.
I loved, you accuse me,
the girth of ugly women
and murmurous waves
the silent bells of diviners
with hanging balls.
My lights, you accuse
had no end
So I must carry Christ's cross
to Golgotha.
I decline, very politely decline,
I decline the unforeseen flame.
For my light I select the sea
and the air, above all the air
so by the miracle of my hand
I shall fashion my own halo
across the bright rays of space.
I shall not pass through Barcelona
or Paris; I will avoid London
and Malmo
Maybe, only maybe
I will weep in the exuberant nights
of my flight like a crocodile
I once knew as I leap
for victory and death

which is all victory and death.
For then I'll come to port
my deck cleansed of all pestilences,
of the phony academics and their murderous accents,
of the beggars clutching their banners
of the soldiers leaning their guns
against the walls awaiting the call
of nights and dawns and days.
I will lie in ambush
for the first governor and his mistress
returning from the party beneath the harbor
Then I shall ground my dream
descend from the space allotted me
to ask the widow a few leading questions
that will help my judges decide my fate.
For I have cut the roses
burnt the lilies
partaken of the feast in foreign lands
of slaughtered goats under Texan almonds
I have danced beneath the shades of bamboos
and sloping alcoves of the Czechoslovak
lady with the dog.
I have saluted the followers of Christ
on San Bernardino where the beggar king
played his guitar to the hippie commune
long jailed for receiving stolen goods
I have cut my muscles on
the punching bags in the karate shop
where the lumpy black belt
heard my fits and cries in the night.
And I am not afraid.

So what else does the gurgling pigeon know?

When Going into Jail

In the dream I arrived, as always
beneath the rock
where stones were quarried
long ago to build our harbor
The bleating of a goat announced
the emergence of a hunter upon the rock
a flint-lock gun and a khaki jacket
with stripes of a forgotten Burmese campaign
Then the lion and a salmon
danced in the shadow of the rock
the music came from the salt flats
of my birthplace
parabolic, immense
the hunter watched the dancers
and went once more
over the hill.

Africa

Once a memory and a song
now a place felt
in the marrow
of the absent bone

Poem

Once more I bleed
on the caramel sheets of Mongolia
suns and curvatures of faces tight lipped
zipper countenances in orbs of golden suns
the bluejays mated under my window
summer of '72 in Kalamazoo
was the last frontier post of my trip
So the players of single string guitars
and ukulele sing of love left long ago
in Latvia where once the spring bloomed
before the coming of the red army.
Can we not know, Do we not find
the tears kept in alabaster vessels
in telephone voices over fathomable
distances? Can we
but see the lines in the infant palms
as he drools and the mother kisses
him? We too will punch divorced apples
under enamel trees
send messages to long forgotten lovers

Of Absence

Now a pattern of the Christian cross
repudiated now
in memory of an infancy
of faith in a sojourning God
winter came first in the Castle

as we searched the sorrows of hand
the glitter of the Bavarian girl
in the drifting field
spreading her wings
for me, oh for me alone
upon a mirror of that heaven
where she said redemption lay
the Norwegian lover and her boots
of snow in Malmo
Guri they call her
yielding from a broken tooth
aches all over
and the floor board in
the house in Malmo
beneath the tram
rattling off to the hills
I would not want to hurt
the lovers of my life.
In Virginia we gathered cartridge
shells of the confederate army
and the drummers from
my village played for me
and Richard and Barbara
for me and Walton
 in the mirror of heaven
 where redemption lay
So I take off to Greenwich Village
to hear the jazz
 Jones at the Gate
 Shepp at the Vanguard
the drummers of my hometown
are here.
 Excuse me. I must go now.

Poem

So he comes now the clown
after the market is closed
and the bells have rung
    a string of tears.
He walks the path alone
behind his father's bier
a scowl on his face
and in his pocket
    a supremely obscene gesture.
Our time came in the morning
the evening was set aside
a boat ride to Bridgeport
the noon a barbecue at Jack's
he knew Berryman who wrote sad poetry
who jumped over a bridge one spring afternoon,
oh ask me about afternoons
tented colors on the fresh colored flowers
in the comradeship of the gardener's failing
nerves; a swim in the sounds
as the gulls watch us, black and white
against the remnant Atlantic
    of my home.
The oliveless martinis, large
and frosty in the cooling wing of the pine
while the one-eyed owl salutes us
from the tennis court
the demons are asleep
then the long tales of the memory
of my slavery days where we danced
beneath chandeliers and the gaslight
spattered like a toothless whore

They say during the siege of Stalingrad
Kruschev hid in a ravine.

Poem

Here I lie
on the Procrustean bed
in the American dream
cut with the meat-cutter's cleaver
in the singsong day of seasons

Sequences

1. small canoe on water
    drifts
    the rower dead
    in the reed
    rain fell on the water
    on leaves
    on reeds green
    now near water
    the canoe came
    to rest
    in the house
    near water
    without the man
    who died in the reed

2. touch me now
    where you used to
    I confess to cruelty
    lying corruption
    fornication and
    happiness
    at times
            in the morning
    singularly enduring
            erections
    but sincerely
            at night by light
    in the deep love
    of my children

3. Some mornings the blue jays

returned, them I knew in Kalamazoo
the hymns end in Bremen
on my ancestral land
where fate seals my heart
in an old jam jar

4. bands on the fields
where death roamed April 67
I warned the soldiers
of death and his treachery
I am steady on my feet
soon I'll need crutches.

5. Our critics say I don't know
the song, the song of this drum
I cannot drum the drum or
dance the dance, the dance
              of this drum this song.

6. Where my song ends
let me start
on the hill
near arcs of light
the memory of death
I died once on 90 W
of a winter and
              greed.
They saw the faces
of my children in the Sea
dead Africans in the passageway
before abolition
among us my children
retrievable shell in my sea
at home now where

I once sang of the land
        where my children live
       like the sea.

7. One gull in flight
   pranks with dragon flies
   on shore homing from fishing
   on oceans
   in time will arrive memorial day
   with twigs for a hut

For Henoga Vinoko Akpalu

who passed away November 1974
(to be read to snatches of his dirges.)

The lagoon, the mat
the eyes upon the earth
despair that none shall come
over the void
to stretch even the short rope
for you on your journey
water, corn flour
wild carnations, the trussed fowl
sacrifice and the tree at the gate.

The road jammed with travelers
hawkers on bicycles
bells ringing and gongs
the road broad streaming.

Then I realized
that some were coming
and others going
all on foot
to the hoot of horns
and the clang of bells
on the road jammed
with travelers

I remember more
the promise
of youth reckless as the
          cultivated beard
sharp pair of trousers
the badly tailored coat

You said once
You said the tear
was the pear of the soul
food for gods at sacrifice
Huge now the platter
like the music of crumbling walls
fools and poets
are the same mother's children.

I fled to America
in blonde pleasures
reliving my cosmopolitan
nay international dreams
new, new man, my voice
my manners
so I lost the faculty
of defecation
with the miracle of the wild lily

I sailed my own ship
to Byzantium to see the youth
for elders in the reversal.
A young man Hasidic to his skull-cap
eyed me nervously
mistaking me I hope for my beard
for a panther. So I march now
with the armies of Caesar on Rome
a companion now of Hannibal
freshly out of Africa *ex Africa aliquid*
semper elephantes
for the alps the alps
Europe the Sartrean negritude
and Dantesque lower region
My Africa the bullshit concentric
    circle
For a song please vomit Blood
in Capetown, murder me Vorster
and Allende in Santiago
For a dance give me Christ Castro's
    head since the Baptist died
of American bullet in Bolivia

Who said the work of man is not done.

An American Poem

Not sensational ephemera
but that deep passionate voice
Kazin claimed for me in Saturday
The conspiratorial voice of Ginsberg

Singing a Hopi chant
in the Stony Brook that was once
    a place of miracles.
I have watched the blue-jays of Kalamazoo
and named them after my dead aunts
Thunder came that noon
in the Library where I'd gone
to check out Virginian history
It took away my voice
discord here on earth
to gain the heaven of all absolutes.
In the Library
a tin tray for my cigarettes
I gave them up one November
Gary and his Zen songs for the citizens
of Alcatraz long reprieved
for a Washington march
singing hail to the Chief
Nixon an incarnate Chippewa
chieftain that sold his tribe
for a wet blanket

Nothing that bursts
in the bright regions of Nogales
will surprise the poets.
Neil Claremon in Tucson
J.D. in Amherst
Jack in Wading River
    Simpson in Belle Terre
and Ethiopia spreads her wings
They say Sellassie was an old man
who once won a war
and fed tidbits to aged lion companions
in Addis Ababa.

Between the sun and my head
a pen of blood rests to write the story
of Negroes hanged in Jackson
black boys shot in Memphis
newly returned from France
and the trenches of Holland
The guns still patrol the streets
        for Law and Order.
Haitian princes
              clubbed in Yankee Boston
power in the horsey land
        dream the pulverized seed
with gin aniseed and mead
the anthropomorphic order
regained now in the covenant of bread.

Liberty, redemption, freedom
from oppression

Our anthems, oh destroyer,
sing our anthems of the pomegranates
the mating of the poinsettias
crocus and jerry lilies in May
in Berkeley of tear gas
and hippie revolt.
Sing of the armadillo's gait
and the dark holes of hung-over mornings
of Middleton coming on a whale
past Labrador.

They cut down the trees of Africa
        the lady said.
Ten Biafran officers
were released yesterday from jail

Israel must live
The Palestinians must live
The old sheiks must live
Sadat must live
Jerusalem must live
    Ford must live
        G.M. must live.

God Bless America.

Another Lover's Song

(for M.K.)

When you went away
    the way the first one went
    Summer in Denver
    Zeke and Rebecca
    holding court
        in the sad sad breathless hills
    where rumor says radioactive
    leak comes to yellow
    the wings of green butterflies
    and the nose of the Chancellor
    the librarian's wife
        lean and asthmatic
            unto death.

In the moon's presence
translucent as our duty
when Norman chose the clothes

for the fashion of our lives.
We relive this night
the wet joy of birth
and cried long
as Julie cried long
    on the Dagomba loom
        of legends

You told me of the trip to Mopti
into the desert
home memory of Cortaro
and the cats and the coyotes
    the crescent moon over the hills
patterns that are blood
sliced now form
upon the mellow land, my love;
We sang that song of Bremen:
He whom the Lord loves
him he sends afar
    to witness his miracles.

Self-Portrait

He read the poem for me at the Y
    after the salutations
    I rush into the hall
    expecting to see the poet.
    With Richard and Mike we rode
    into the sea at night
    You must see the Texan sea
        at night.

Item: a fishing pole
Item: a bowl of shrimps (we ate it for lunch)
Item: one lost African
     in Texas with his friends

So much for the moon
and the drummers now
for the lovers kissing in the bar
and the prostitute girl I loved
beneath my window
singing my name
please open the door for me
The refrain runs through 40 years
Elijah needed in the wilderness
Where are my lizards in the hill?
Someone cooked them they say

Someone in Mopti stewed
them with barks dressed
them in non-fat milk packed tight
in Milwaukee (where I once had a girl)
once she insisted on keeping her skirt on
when she took them off later
underneath were poems
reams of poems she wanted to read.

PART TWO

Homecoming ... Poems from Prison

Homecoming

Much
   marked
in the margin of our life
so this winged forlorn hope
burns and sustains
   always.
The eternal pain resolves
in the swollen eye
the cut on the forgotten elbow.

God looks over us.

We seek no more
the singular beauty
of victory
   and death
death wipes out
the red blushes of the rose
the curvature of the thistle's neck
the rings on the desert tree.

So I reject death now
   as counterproductive
   terminal and deadly
I chose the hills
   and the sea nearby.

The Second Circle

Beginning Midnight 5/1/76

(5th January 1976)

Cell No.2

They say those about to drown
always see their entire life
flash before them.
It did not happen to me
So I will not drown.

Fear,
for friends, comrades,
but never for yourself
because your death cannot
matter very much to you,
Can it now?

So much does a little bird know
about the world.
So much.

in the still hour of the night
I dream of fliers and conjurers
I met a little flyer
in the fields.
Where are you heading, I asked
Don't you know?
Home.

On Being Told of Torture

For each hair on man, there is
a ledger in which the account
    will be written.
Time is not measured by the hourglass
but by the rivulets of blood
      shed
    and will be shed
Even though our bones crunch
Our spirits will not break
  until we make a
    reckoning in the red bright book
      of history.

He said he saw him lying
on the floor in his own blood
      unconscious
  delirium was his refuge
  from pain. In that state,
  my mother will bear arms
  and urge me to topple a govt.
  But, no matter what,
  there is still a tree blossoming
  now this New Year,
  there is goodwill on earth
    children still laugh
      lovers hold hands in dark corners,
    and the moon is new on all of us.

Weep not now my love
for as all die, so shall we
but it is not dying that should pain us.

It is the waiting,
      the intermission when we cannot act,
   when our will is shackled by tyranny.

That hurts.
Yet somehow, I know
the miracle of the world
will be wrought again,
  the space will be filled
  in spite of the hurt
  by the immensity of love
  that will defy dying
    and Death
       Good night, my love.

The First Circle

1.
  the flat end of sorrow here
two crows fighting over New Year's Party
leftovers. From my cell, I see a cold
     hard world.

2.
So this is the abscess that
  hurts the nation—
    jails, torture, blood
      and hunger.
  One day it will burst;
    it must burst.

3.

When I heard you were taken
we speculated, those of us at large
where you would be
in what nightmare will you star?
That night I heard the moans
wondering whose child could now
be lost in the cellars of oppression.
Then you emerged, tall, and bloody-eyed.

It was the first time
      I wept.

4.

    The long nights I dread most
    the voices from behind the bars
  the early glow of dawn before
the guard's steps wake me up,
the desire to leap and stretch
and yawn in anticipation
of another dark home-coming day
only to find that
    I cannot.
  riding the car into town,
hemmed in between them
    their guns poking me in the ribs,
    I never had known that my people
    wore such sad faces, so sad
    they were, on New Year's Eve,
    so very sad.

Dream of Home

I used to lie, wherever I lay,
and dream of home; of the spot I
stood at once to proclaim mine,
a banana tree was once there.
The fragrance of the talcum on my aunts
fresh from the wash,
the coming of new babies
all ours;
time itself draped all
in indigo, the colors clear
suns, burning suns, bright
   days and nights.

Revolution

We must use our brains
for it is better to die
      than lie awake
however is the mind bare
the hungry people, the
army of beggars and
the soldiers with shooting
      and swagger sticks.
Why must we be afraid of cannons
   and rains?
For death by any means is
   Death.

But our death must be
	Birth,
a trip to the blossoming of fruit trees
overabundance of rice,
the overweight of the plantain
the eternal season of fish,
is the building of roads,
schools, hospitals, homes for
the aged, orphanages for love children
	and love.

For then we shall have died
	as heroes,
		only then.

To Sika on Her 11th Birthday

Tomorrow, my love
You will turn eleven.
I had promised a party;
But worry not. I won't be there.
Your mother will give you a party
Tell me if she doesn't.
Where am I? Well, very near you.
But there are iron bars on my door;
a man stands there with a gun
He brings me food and water
now and then.
And I dream, that soon,
	You and I and all of us
		will be free!

At times the vision of victory
comes so blurred and dim. So much is a haze, uncertainty.
But somehow in this frame flickers a little light which keeps
on the search, a veritable instrument around which
hope settles, quietly, stirring now slumbering now, but
hanging on, just hanging on.

Ussher Fort Prison, 26 February 1976

What does he mean by moral solitude? Perhaps a singular effort
to withdraw into a world where you can seek communication with
your inner self, to make contact with a form you once dreamt you
had reached, to shatter, as it were, the whole grid of a past sensibil-
ity for the reconstruction of a new ego based on a new insight, and
a faith regained.

Ussher Fort Prison

Revolution

A Chat with Ho Chi Minh's Ghost

Ho: Nothing is more precious than independence and liberty.

Me: True, Uncle, but in the aftermath of liberty
nothing can be more precious than a full life
infinite use of our capacity and the ability to hope
and dream, and be ourselves.

Ho: Correct, my son. That is what liberty means.

Me: And the possibility of being murdered in a dark cell?

Ho: Yes. That is what liberty, infinite liberty means for a true
    revolutionary.

Me: I see, now.

    Hot nights
  meals tossed in gray pans
  on the blotched floor.
  A distinct smell of the sea.
You remember the arc of birds
    the sharp teeth of the bluefish on Chesapeake
    the wing of the chattering bluejays of Kalamazoo.

plants now in season
    in the land
dryness of harmattan, respite
    of dust. Honor, a diadem
    we wore once young
As now in age we anticipate
    life, here, on this shore
in this shore house
    now home at home
    where my heart dreamed to grow
Captive residuary nerves
    atrophied by exile
in the magic pain and mystery of an alien sky

The birds will fly back soon.
They will remind me of leftovers
of rainy nights of insects
    and the drum of rains
    over the voices of 400 captives.

Ussher Fort Prison, 16 February 1976

Much here the tinker said
and the cobbler slept

For the best sleep visit a jail
the citadel of premeditated madness
      futile gestures of defiance
      boots applied to earthbound heads
      blood on the pavement near the communal kitchen
      so close to the open air latrines.

All represent the ivy's bend
its pointed needle.
I saw a crow on the latrine wall
we were told to use water
      as no tissues have been delivered from HQ

The crow was agitated.
      It had a limp
      It hopped on the roof
      beneath him tattered blinds
      blow in the little wind.
It took a brief look at us
      and fled
Then there were four swallows
dancing in the bluest jail sky
I ever saw in drifts
of swift arks
      now dark dots against
      my ache.
They vanished over the distant wall.

      And my heart
            once mutinous
            under the weight of hurts

```
seeks a place
        any place—
beneath a dripping tree
on a windswept beach
on a bright April sky
a place—
        any place
                of birth.


And my tree will blossom
        on the beach
        of an April day
to crumble this wailing will.
```

Most acts of goodness return in the long hours of
sleep, boredom, my steadiest companion. I am striving for
some inner peace. It involves philosophy, mystery, the
universe and God. Whatever these mean, they represent an
array of external intangibles upon which thought can rest (in
lieu of action). And the focus <u>can</u> be created for a better life.

It is Sunday, the noisiest day in our jail.

Ussher Fort Prison, 22 February 1976

Found Poem

In the east, the day breaks; do not
say we have started too early;
For we shall cross many hills yet
Before we grow old; here
    the land is surpassing in beauty.

Mao Tse Tung 1934

I look out the bars upon the Castle
    the crust caked row of age
    in a corner my friendly spider
    crouches for the unwary gnats
    of my days.

    So much there is we must atone.
There are spires of faith
in the invisible claws of spiders
in the flight and curve of gulls.
These know, I swear,
    the contours of the rolling Saharas
    and the destitute oceans of our history.
We sit, debating the charity of our captors.

At night lights come on
the shoreline bends into a broad bay
    near the Castle
    the sea is gray
Yesterday it rained on the eve
    of my forty-first year
      and left all my defeats intact

Let me lead you into the country
It is only as half clansman
    of the ritual goat
that I bring my song to the place of sacrifice
here in the pain fields
    asphalt and smoke of a large hearth
I lead
my rope is short.
    I shall soon arrive under the tree.

I will stage a hundred fights in honor of our Gods
and our beloved leader
Here, I could care less for the toiling masses
I retreated here before Lent
to my own stretch of sea front
(I cannot see the damned sea
    because of old caked walls
    built by Dutchmen)
But the shore falls into a deep gulf
    there are no cliffs.

They found a week-old baby
buried in a shallow grave
on the front lawn of the fort.
I want my grave to be deeper.

They are sawing through our firewood
   Today is cassava day
The flutist is silent
Perhaps his troops have arrived in Georgia

Not to arrive upsets me
And for the path that I have trod
   I have no regrets

Another Found Poem

So deep the night, so slow to break the crimson dawn
Demons and ghouls held sway so many centuries
Like desert sand, our hapless downtrodden people;
Then the cock crowed
And suddenly all our heavens clear in the light
And from Khotan to ocean sounds of music
Setting the poet's mind aglow with dreams.

Mao Tse Tung

I dream of a sun-drenched beach
of an afternoon of open fields
   fishermen at song
   lovers hurrying to their meeting place
   a bird
   alone
   vaulting the blue of a sky
   shrieking for his girl
   across the world, alone
     sad
        and free

Ussher Fort Prison, 28 March 1976

It is possible to become sentimental
   we must not overdo it
   not crucify the flapping wings of remembrance
   for today's sun as it surely sets
   will usher in another sun tomorrow
   and that's a commonplace and a cheap opinion
     if you ask me.

but he will come blazing
bringing his own gifts of love
    and memories
    of hate
in the thistle prick of roses
  the dying cry of gulls
in the rushing wind
of the open country
    of the native land.

Ussher Fort Prison, 30 May 1976

In a prison yard they crushed
the petals of our being
against a long row of ancient walls and
a line of assorted flowers.

but there is stillness here
which is crammed full of bits
of history executioners heroes condemned men
on such a day
  who would dare think of dying?

So much Freedom means
that we swear we'll postpone dying
until the morning after.

Ussher Fort Prison, 24 April 1976

A solitary moon
a host of swallows
a blazing jet trail
against a fading blue sky.
Very soon it will be lock-up time.

Ussher Fort Prison, 9 May 1976

The Place

You remember sometimes
that the place is by the sea,
And once in a while you see a gull
    rise
    swift against the blazing sun
    in dazzling colors playing
in the shards of a noonday.
It's always so swift, so brief
At night you recall it all
while the door is locked.

Poem

I have found my domain
at last; in the sarcophagus
of the blood
We plunge into a new darkness
Usurp the heavy hand of our only godhead
in the cannibal meal of fetus
the horror of the sacrament of pork
luring us into the chthonic
where we wait.

Us

Who are we here
but timekeepers in the house by the sea,
watching for the dawning sounds
the mildest inflection in the announcer's voice
We clutch our hopes like pebbles

scoured by infants
with eyes on the northern shore
as we trail behind the gulls
Only we do not see the beach
    nor the shore

Love

Stay for me there, stay for me
So the world becomes a prayer
A vast precious jewel
    You
the crystal light of life here
    dissolves
shimmering in its last ecstasy
of long day dawn triumph of pain
      on this brink

Personal Note

What am I doing
who am the liar in the academy
verdicted by the Prosecutor
in this peculiar hour of Truth.
How much is there in the weight of love?
So little.

What matters is the sun in the morning
the splitting of the drink
in memory
the willingness to die
in snowfields near a desert
of history ravaged
by a savage instinct
that lurks in the rose or the gun
the brutal smile of spastics
the symbol of hope of the nation
Soon to be our sword and shield.
However
the ceremony must wait
till we've tilled the land
ploughed over this harvest of tears
erect proper fences to keep out
the sorrow and the sorrowers
prepare new sowing songs
arm our songs with the blade
and the handle of love
in the steel vigor of the iron;
So that ravaging her once more
we plant her, sow
her fields once more with other tears.

Sea Time, Meaning a Pledge

for Kojo Tsikata sentenced to death by firing squad

I hear the thuds again.
They just brought me a smuggled egg
   I ate it and afterwards
     belched.

The sea pelts the land
with grains of fine drops
   very cold, this August
some were talking of dying
of petitions and reprieves
Ousman speaks of his horse
He's been a thief all his life.

In 48 they held a victory dance
belatedly and I
as a boy drank too much.

We come now to the house
by the sea, to the ferry port
   Companioned by gulls
and the shouts of naked boat men
   deserters and watchmen
     at many shrines

The wisdom that my father had
is not passed. I dreamt
my grandmother mocked me
as I led a tattered procession
of women and children

to seek a reprieve on a road.
Go and tell them
that my passion is ended
that my love I gave away
that I need no braves
on the ferry. That if need be
   I'll row it alone
   We already spoke of cannons
   and roses; of death
   and tree gardens
   of love and milk in prison
   of an egg and tiger nuts.

I come alone into the city
   all are gone to ferry port.
Alone here, I wander among ghosts
of soldiers who died in domestic wars
Alone I sing of cannons
and rain among the memory of slaves
of life and fruit trees
hunger in alleyways
and tears, abundant tears
(oh, when shall I sing of joy alone?)

But I promise a harvest
unheard of; I promise a garland
for your wounded knees
(the ones you gained when you fell
   in the communal bathhouse)
a crown of thorns is too common
who needs a crown of thorns?

They promised me they'll come into the city
with me. They swore

They'll lead me to the festival grounds
for I have a pledge to make
I'll make it
before death comes.

My smuggler is offering eggs
I need many eggs.

The Will to Die

In memory of Allotey who died in my cell on the 2nd of March, 1976

What is this will we claim
in arguments
against pain, silence
or hope?
So our silence will sing
with the daylight gong
a dirge at birth time
that in love we rise
to go to the ferryport
long deserted in dreams.
We place our headloads
on the platform
to await our friend
and ferryman.

Those expecting us
we see them waving.

They make us live,
our love longing for home
is heard
in this river, our river
this valley, our valley
this land, our land.

Where are all the people gone?

A Little Word

1.
I wrestle with my white angel
among flower beds in prison.
Prison cats are my witnesses.

2.
buck you up
upon this triumph
appalled by all the free
 and the dead

in the weird regattas
 this afterwards
all those afterworlds

3.
 all my territories
 across the Volta
I wanted to plant them.
Instead I plait my hope

into poems
the sounds I make here
part of the landscape
    of my new homeland

4.
it is not meant for mad men
    this passion
marinated for an overnight
drive across my desert
kept fresh in sealed jars
    this lament.

Ussher Fort Prison, August 1976

Today on the eve of Monday
today I'll be in court again.
I feel happy.
It's a bit chilly
They are frying groundnuts
My cell has just been locked
by a friendly warder
He spoke to me of courage
manliness and
        gave the story of a monkey
            who took the bullet
                on his chest.
        I must not neglect my duty.

Ussher Fort Prison, August 1976

The Wayfarer Comes Homes

(A poem in five movements)

For Naana in remembrance of her
    devotion and love
For Joseph Bruchac and my comrades in America
Whose concern I'll always cherish

I. THE PROMISE

Even here in my cell
in the house of Ussher
I hear the guns.
They are killing the children of Soweto
  Even now
    as the southern winter ends
    and the first heat of Africa
    steadies itself for a journey,
    the children of Africa die.
It is not only the guns
Of Vorster you hear.
Listen again, carefully.
Then I heard a wren
in the morning of the alley sun
  Sing.
It is a long time since
I heard a bird cry.

So I came into the city alone
having walked the listening shore
where the salmon and the turtle store
their love among the water willows.

Of a sinning time I've already confessed
    abundantly. I rest now in my days of quietude.

What animals eat here
on this disastrous shore?
What says this bleak storm
in the fathomable wave of my river?

I love I love I love,
not the wispy geranium or the lily
but the curvature of your arms
the fragrance of your armpit after the rain
where the seed our son hides
waiting to be born.
I too have come home to be born
in the wake of the seed.
In the single way journey upon the sea.
My companions the flying fish
    heading toward the coast of Senegal.
    We rode, we rode
    taking the waves
    as we traced the Middle Passage backward
    in the smell of vomit
    our light bent for home
    gray in the August moon.

I sang of the sea of my love,
of you, home and invisible woman
whom I've known since conception
though you were lost once
among the high grass of infancy.
I searched for you in foreign lands
in the faces of strangers in the cities of the Europe
on the subways of Manhattan

in the dripping trams of Chicago.
I searched for you among the picnic crowds
in Santa Barbara and Babylon
and once I thought I saw you
on the horizon in Texas or Louisiana
between Corpus Christi and Baton Rouge,
another time on the crowded train
between Tokyo and Hiroshima.

But you were another spirit
of another time and place.
You were the tired salmon
after the torrent time of the river
   But like the spirit
     and the fish
You swam on upon your journey.
You remain the visible flame of youth
the interstice between birth and dying,
the heady era of stolen drinks and kisses.

Will it be enough now
that I sing you, my love
in the slave fort of Ussher
the sun bleary eyed this September morning
annoyed dopey sulking
   in a corner of history's last day?
Will it be enough
that I cry for you my love
of nights in solitary
in my vast cell
listening to the prison cats in heat?

Oh how needless are all our days
and hours spent cutting our nails

spent dreaming of victory.
How futile the child's request in the night
when he knows
he seeks the impossible

So we share companionship
   with evil animals
      our fellow travelers in a leaky canoe.

I was once king of the mountain
I mean the range that stretches across Togo.
I was the lion that roamed the violent shores.
The Volta was a river of passion then
And in the valley Datsutagba
history was made by ancestral spears.
I was once the ferryman of the river.
   But now I weep now
   in a slave cell
   remembering only the whisper of your face
   the abundance and multitude of your promise

   Is it enough
that the children of the mountain
   and the salt waters
   die in a storm in a leaky canoe?
It is enough
   the valley's lost its shimmer
   on this sultry September day?

II. THE SUN'S MERCY

death tramp the stalking
animal shall die
Shall die shall die

death tramp beat the earth
smash the mirror
smash the man
the evil animal shall die
   shall die
I prefer death to joy
I have known drums weep
in the Yewe celebration
the milkbush shed tears in response
the leopard saw the lion on the path,
both, in a warrior gait
salute the land in a rear.
The leopard and the lion met
in the valley. The grass bore witness.

There is death in the land
there is death in the land
The leopard is in the forest
He was lured to the rivershore
There he met an evil foe
Their fight is still the fight remembered.

Come and touch me
Come with your claws unfurled
Come that you and I roll in this valley.

You cannot count the seeds
without cracking the gourd.
The circle fire simply does not go out
There are seeds in the ancient gourd.
Touch my hand
and I will tell you your fate.

Gbedzi gbedzi gbedzi

gbedzi gaga, gbedzi
Ga wo fui de go
fiawo fui de go
Nye medu So fe nu
Ne So na wum e.
Vo neto dzi, Vo neto dzi, Vo neto dzi.

III. THE SEED

In my grandfather's farm
when we were boys
there roamed an old alligator.
Grandfather said he was harmless
if only we kept the eggs away from him.
Slow, deliberate, slightly stupid
he paid heed to our going and coming.
One great flood time of Aka our river
and the alligator was seen no more.

In the remembrance of death
we renew the primal oath
that we like our palms
shall yield fruit before dying.
I remember walking the lanes
of the village of my birth
saluting all in a long salutation.
An old red man offered me
a piece of smoked hawk.
My mother said he was a wizard
so I drank palm oil
to throw up the smoked hawk.
I vomited more than
the piece of smoked hawk.

So we will seek refuge
in the corners of history
like the squirrels of Sofe
Where drums are still
  and the fences broken
Where muffled voices
heard at dawn
turn ululations of burial processions.
Where the single orphan
covered with yaws roams the dunghills
an outcast in his native town
red with the red of the earth.

Once I knew the crackle of the pod
the report startling and brief
registering more that a fact of botany
more than a statement of fact.

The lily and the wild crocus are still;
the cemetery flowers droop
over the earthen graves
(here we do not cover the dead in concrete)
for the fertility time
and the magical aid of the seed.
We leave the dead alone
to return to us at dawn
  at seedtime
in the abundance of the earthly harvest.
They the dead diet for worms
and kinsmen of the shadowy earth
in the embrace of the sun
as they trail in the valley
and in the mountain.
Their muffled voices proclaim
benedictions for all

in the dark of the earth at noon.
I ran again in their wake
cavort to the somersault of the rhythm
perform the funeral dance of notables
in my brief cloth.
They clapped for me, the elders
They clapped for me, child of the valley
and the mountain; they claim
for me the moon
birds and the fish
in their high leaps
in the wake of the lover land.

What is this hunger of which you die
in the midst of harvests
gathered by your own hands?
For the brief glory of the land
raise up a song for the lover
    create anthems of praise
for we soon shall tire of symphonic disasters
    shall weary of the lingering sun
on a bleak September day.

My soul stands at the gate
lonely, waiting
He carries a flag and a pod
waiting. His gait spare
precise clothed in a shroud of glory
adorned by the touch of a formal flame.
This lion of light and fire
burns on this corridor of history
oblivious of the coming showers of October
exhaling the enormous whiffs
of the burning harmattan bush
    waiting.

On a clear day
you can see all the houses of Anyako
across the salt lagoon
You can hear the drums roll
down the water to the sea.

   On a clear day
you can see the fishers idle
   upon the shore

   The seed's ardour
is the miracle of birth
   the quickening pulse of the reckoning moment
   defiance is the magic of the seed
   birth is the ultimate celebration
so the hollow oak hides only seeds
   a million thousand seeds
   ready to be scattered
      over the dreary earth

So I wipe away my tears
on the outskirts of the village
I tie my cloth tighter
on the threshold of the shrine
I steady myself for the dance
   In this lovely seed time.

IV. ECHOES

Wayfarer, alone now
upon the road,
rest now near the copse
near the cleavage in the hill
for rest calls you now.

Stop awhile on the journey home
Your soul waits on the trail
of hunters, in the wake of harvesters.
What wearies your body
at this subliminal hour?
Come near the circular fire,
in this strange village
they will give you to eat
   and water your tired feet.
Though strangers, wayfarer,
  they understand the thirst
    in your throat, the hunger and fire
  in your belly
Let your cripple's crawl
  change into a warrior's gait
and dance the ancient dance of notables
The land your lover
  waits for you
its valleys greeny in September
its mountains blue beyond heaven.
She waits trailing her marriage gown
white, her headgear indigo
her necklace of precious beads
in a circlet of red.
She stands out there
  on the outskirts of a native village
    crying softly for joy

She stands out there
in the midst of old glories
waiting for your homecoming

Wayfarer, you who knows
the shape of every rock on this mountain,

the texture of every leaf in this valley,
You who have measured with your tears
  every weary mile.

Your companions are the sparrow's aunt
the eagle's father
and the wild cock's concubine
You have shared a laugh with the hyena
a handshake with the monkey
and hooted back at the deep-eyed owl at dusk.
Every blade of grass knows the weight
  of your footfall, every wind
    the smell of your sweat
Come now, hurry home
follow the echo of your natal sounds
follow the call of the wren
and the evening bell cry of the pigeon dove.
Hurry on home, wayfarer
leave the sooty cities of the evil animal.

I have learnt to listen to the evening
to sit quietly by my bed of mercy
  waiting for you to come home.
I have learnt to count evening shadows
at noon, to signify the enormity of my fate
in the enclosure of my hands.
In the rains yesterday
I wished to dance again
the dance I did in youth
I wished for the sun this September day
to embrace the old slaves my comrades of this fort
whose ghosts torment my sleep.
In solitary I brood over the cats
and the flowers outside
I count the iron bars in the overhead cage

The flowers weep, wayfarer
Come home now to the mountain
Come to the greeny valley
Come dance with me
    at our jubilee; Laugh again
Your ancient laugh. You know
our gods are maimed
by native and foreign cudgels
muffled yet stout their voices remain
to proclaim the festival
of your homecoming.

Here, in this brief corridor of desolation
in this concrete yardage of pain
we snatch little joys in remembrance
of a place once where the baby lay
of the pleasure at the mourner's ululation.
Here the tumult has barely died down
where the sun proclaimed a respite
  symbolic gestures of a tired man
    revealed now as
      great truths and visions
        long known, terrible presentiments
          shrinking with tidal turns, reckonings.

I pause for breath, wayfarer
I pause for a brief benediction

V. ONE ALONE: THE BIRD SWEEPS

At the first journey, at dawn
the sea emerges. Some call her mad
She yields to the land of pure sand
beautiful beyond recalling.
On clear days, the eye

can sweep across the old plantation
maintained once by slave labor
its harvest long buried in history
the grandeur of this land
defies poetry and music
But they still sing of her
in long voluminous poems
in elaborate symphonies
There is rhythm of course
as you cannot talk
of this land without rhythm.

Evening is the time for fires
the cowherds driving their wards across the grassland
fishermen sharing the last catch;
each gesture a caress, an embrace
of this lover land.
The long last light bursts
upon the houses made of branches,
the light wind steadies the flicker
of the oil lamps
as they burn in the naked twilight.

Beyond this lies deep penetration of forests
home for gnomic tendencies
and tribal mysteries;
they embrace mountains and hills
   we call them mountains for we love them
   circular immense yet fragile
   splendid like pubertal dances.
   They state the reality of love
   the claims of kinship
They too sing their dark jubilee
   near forgotten villages
longing for the abundant time.

What can I say of you now
You whose mystery keeps me in hope
intangible cause that depicts the effect,
    the love that put me to sea?
What can I say of you now?
You state the wizardry of my loins
    The certainty of my despair,
My heart clothed in a torn jumper
    leaps to be delivered
        from this ineffable pain

Mother, mother, my mother
the hearth is cold
the house is empty
the people are all gone

But I raise up now
the dying animal of love.
The sun proclaims me a claimant
to an ancient stool
releases me from all foreign vows.
The wind the sea and the forest stress
the proclamation of the rain
and the light enunciates
the inexorable tenderness

I love you, I love you
tatters and all. I shield you
with my pain.
I seek release from diseases
so I can bring you cure.
Take away this fatigue of the soul,
send a message to Soweto
on my behalf.
Tell them the festival time is come

that the heap slags of the raw cities
will burn,
that the dance has begun
the drummers all in place;
this dreary half life is over
our dream will be born at noon.
The night is for plots and stratagems.
We shall harness the flames for the revolt
pride shall lead us into armories

We shall stalk the evil animal
   a hundred years times ten hundred
   even beyond the moon.
We abjure all malice
We claim the sanctity of the ambush
   and clean revenge.
We love the smell of dead animals.

In this hour before victory
trace me every line on the dragonfly
count me the legs of the spider hen
the various tongues of water
   and the criss cross of the wind.

Tell me how often the baboon fornicates
how frequent the mountains breathe.
The fish says I know his hiding place
Already the gull's island is my treasure store
Gemi and Amu, mountain and river
Shift the stress upon my heart.

So I make this journey now;
there will be no detours
I shall live on rawhide and locusts

I shall drink of the only wine you serve
   and in the ugly hour long ordained
I shall grind my knife.

I will have no trophies to show
For the swamp beneath the hills
   shall receive the evil animal.

Ussher Fort Prison, 17–22 September 1976

From *Ride Me, Memory*   1973

America

A name only once
crammed into the child's fitful memory
in malnourished villages,
vast deliriums like the galloping foothills of the Colorado:
of Mohawks and the Chippewa,
horsey penny-movies
brought cheap at the tail of the war
to Africa. Where indeed is the Mississippi panorama
and the girl that played the piano and
kept her hand on her heart
as Flanagan drank a quart of moonshine
before the eyes of the town's gentlemen?
What happened to your locomotive in Winter, Walt,
and my ride across the prairies in the trail
of the stage-coach, the gold-rush and the Swanee River?
Where did they bury Geronimo,
heroic chieftain, lonely horseman of this apocalypse
who led his tribesmen across deserts of cholla
and emerald hills
in pursuit of despoilers,
half-starved immigrants
from a despoiled Europe?
What happened to Archibald's
soul's harvest on this raw earth
of raw hates?
To those that have none
a festival is preparing at graves' ends
where the mockingbird's hymn
closes evening of prayers
and supplication as
new winds blow from graves

flowered in multi-colored cemeteries even
where they say the races are intact.

Harlem on a Winter Night

Huddled pavements, dark,
the lonely wail of a police-siren
moving stealthily across
gray alleys of anonymity
asking for food either
as plasma in hospital jars
escaping fires in tenements
grown cold and bitter
seeking food in community garbage cans
to escape its eternal nightmare.
Harlem, the dark dirge of America
heard at evening
mean alleyways of poverty
dispossession, early death
in jammed doorways and creaking elevators,
glaring defeat in the morning
of this beautiful beautiful America.

Long Island Sketches

i.
Single-minded a scholar in slit pants
discoverer of pinafores and modesty
in open jars of beet and cooked asparagus

his cats were his friends to whom he read
bad verse and moral lessons
and dreams of professional ethics and salvation
for poor pedlars of literary jokes.

ii.
Alien here among these muddied fields
Spring showers that wash not away our sins
forgotten now in crammed bunkered rooms
among books and pencil shavings.
New gods are enthroned in our wing
who too will swill noble blood of lost lambs
make bad jokes about blacks and guineas
and stick out finally and irrevocably for the
rights and hopes of all minorities.

iii.
Still pretty at forty, a husband in California
demonic dancer, the frenzy and despair of all parties;
for her fulfilment is the cherubic son
precocious like a deity, and the passion,
of youth. What moves you in these dreary fields,
the agony of the picked rose or the whine
of the jailed salamander?
There will still be the magic in her eyes,
memories of the husband in flowered shirts
and the ancestral desire to do good by all men.

iv.
It was the day Cambodia was invaded
radical causes in geometric progression,
power, no more to the people, died
in the marching tramps of academics
circling Smithhaven mall,

veritable Joshuas without trumpets
or a song. What other grounds shall they hallow
with their gutless cynical blunderings,
these fools dancing at their own execution?

v.

The Brooklyn drunk wheeling through a Puerto Rican market
    place
proclaiming Love it or Leave it
beside Japanese gardens of apples, pears, and pimentos
and blue wine in cellophane jars
The one-legged veteran from Vietnam after seasons of
    Washington
        protests
confessed he lost his leg in an auto crash on *lie.*
Tomato patch on his coat, he fingers his medallions—six of them
and swore he was going to write a poem
full of eternity peace and
        forever.

vi.

He was the boss, this short creature of our pity now
they wheel him in stuffed with influenza
his chest wheezing like a grandfather pipe organ.
Some swore the malevolence hasn't quite left him
for they caught him one May noon on a park bench
eating ten hero sandwiches, and drinking from a mug
swearing secret oaths under his bad breath
of how he will do everyone in
if he regains power.

vii.

The proclamation came first
in pencil. You must address me doctor.

Puzzled beyond words I send polite inquiries
doctor of what? Of letters, words,
oral examinations, course works,
brilliant essays on Hopkins and Eliot, a masters thesis
on Pound the renegade, and above all
a dissertation on the elaborate and unconventional
use of the comma in the poetry
of C. C. Razoogakool the poet laureate of Toogaloo
who in 1864 single-handedly defected to the Federal side
and saved the country and his letters for the world
of tomorrow and the day before tomorrow.
      Long live all PhDs. They are the salt of the earth.

viii.
Love she bears infinitely in her eyes
concerned about my sins and welfare
I suffer the terror of our meeting
I keep on fleeing from her solicitous generosity
from her arms full of spring anemones and fading jasmines
she swore she collected from suburban doorways in Bel Terre.
What can I offer in return for your faith?
A crown of thunder and the garment of chameleons
so that like the Creator God's sister
you will escape change, age, and death?
Let me seek refuge in the knowledge
that come next August I shall be very far away
and you can cook those goddam flowers
and if you can't eat them, stuff them up.

ix.
I have always wondered why
he insisted on staring so hard at me
especially on hot noons on his way to lunch.
I grin, smile, show my flashing cannibal teeth

just to put him on his way. But he hangs on
his arms stretched across my doorway
asking the same questions a thousand times.
My horrible lack of courage is becoming proverbial
but one of these days I will stare sternly back
and in an ominous cannibal African voice I will say
"You creep, move one step and I will break your ugly body
across my knees and stuff your shirt in your stupid mouth
and kick your ass to kingdom come."
Just as the thought was done
the arms reached out for my door that comic book smile
"What are you doing for supper?"
"Nothing," I said, smiling grinning my silly African cannibal smile.

To My Uncle Jonathan

A Song of Abuse

Sir, you stink.
Your red nose is covered with fifty ugly warts.
You are a hairy bastard without a father.
My father sent to tell me how you are walking my beaches
in Bermuda shorts and cursing my sacred name.
You fucker of sheep and goats,
a pederast in bloomers,
a whiskered fool with an obscene mouth.
What wrong did I do you and you curse my name?
I refuse even to touch your stinking daughter
that lean-assed whorelet you sent to my home the other night
the bitch temptress, smelling of mayonnaise and pastrami.
I threw her out, for I am a man of dignity and respect.

If you don't respect my name, others do.
And one other thing, you asked me to call you uncle
You said, "Call me uncle, boy!"
in that stage voice
I heard in Bobo and Lusaka,
So you have joined revolutions now,
gun running for the reds in Siam
piloting fighter planes in Saigon
drinking gin and vermouth in Guatemala
tequila in Puerto Rico.
O my uncle Jonathan, you sent for me.
When I came you left word that you had gone to the wars
that I should drink a glass of bourbon, eat a cake,
and get my ugly mug out of town before you return.
But I like it here. I want to stay awhile.

To Felicity, a Girl I Met in LA

Felicity you are fat,
You are stuffed with hogs and sheep
who now grunt and bleat in your large bosom,
rolling hills without entrance or exit.
Felicity, I hear you've learnt a new laughter
since we last met—a shrill low moan
interlarded with wheezing jerks of far flowing in valleys
Go to a farm, lose weight, Felicity
fat freezes the seminal fluid of giants
congeals the heart-warming desire of braves and stalwarts
and hides the entrance to kingdoms of joy.
Besides, Felicity, it is not good for your heart.
P.S.: Have you learnt to wash your girdles?

Hymns of Praise, Celebration, and Prayer

i.
That strange border town of my mind
between friendship and high esteem
the adoration of the feast and cleaning blood
on this desecrated ground; the ailing grain
of sand in the teeth of time,
awaiting a communal extraction
the celebration of an eagle's flight
    A band of noisy music men will pass through town again
    Hail, the helper, salutations to you all.

ii. *To Dennis Brutus*
At first from your verse
the imprecise dilettante
a cocky troubadour, professional exile,
chronicler of sirens knuckles and boots
through Texan nights
and Lousiana plains, in jazz-halls
and strip-joints, beneath spinning buttocks
    of dancing girls warm
beyond the stars' surmising, a warrior
without a country, a rain cloud
falling in alien lands, a rainbow
of arched serpents
a revolutionary in necktie,
friend of Shakespeare, Wordsworth
and the sirens of your Cape
that will sing you home on rainbows
    someday. I will reiterate your mortality
    when our bones and spirits will not crunch.

iii.

Have I not known the agonies
outlined in the shape of these hills,
the spite of huntsmen lost travelers
trekking back from over alien fields?
I have known the songs of street peddlers
old men in tired native garments and robes,
lonely monitors of an age without a name
whose voices the gods of the south assumed
trumpets in unison here
where our path is smooth
and death is certain at noon
and the nation dies upon her knees
in purple gowns beneath blazing suns
putrescent blood beating
our drums of doom.

iv.

behind the barricades of hills
and roses, the summer months
and sorrow returning hand over head
after burying her husband in Minneapolis
fleeing the enchantress bull dyke
heroine of Korea and Hue
now a shrill feminist in liberation hats
campaigning for non-heroes in Milwaukee.
        What prophecies do you carry in your milk
        down these trails watering national fields and flowers?
Was there not a dirge sung at Arlington
and Memphis? What new hymns do you start
here behind sea-stars and agonized dragon-eyes
and flies?
        Where there are gods of war there must be gods of peace.

v.

Our climb through the aloes
last trails to the house of the August moon
ten thousand yards of creek, bleached water
is Winnipeg and the ashen prairie
dog, cousin of the coyotes and the toothy wolf;
there attending the official grand ball of the salmons
in water caverns, the deer the gatemen,
ending among hills dancing a jubilee;
for my levitation erect a crown of thunder
the booming elephant my trombonist
of god's own green acres shall join
when sun moon and I, march cousins,
and destiny's relatives in our dance
again, another millennium.

vi. *The Coral Isle, the Lion-coloured Sand Burst*
In Upon the Porcelain Revelry.

Ezra Pound (The Age Demanded)

The mythical meeting of the salamander and the man
creation's princess and its agony
form a circlet around this ball of fire
which is his name;
and his majesty.

vii.
Yesterday the cry was Biafra
yesterday noon it was Bangladesh
a million Bengalis on Pakistani swords
blood in the fertile rice bowl of the Ganges
while ages heave sighs in useless assemblies
Yahya Khan's nose is Nero's fiddle

played upon by scents of burning incenses
and the Krishna swore Mohammed was a bigot,
a felonious war-monger in women's clothes
a holy assassin in the name of Allah
the Beautiful as there is only one God Allah
and Mohammed is his prophet
    keep away from hogs
Kali the bare-breasted goddess, the Baghavad Gita in the hands
   of
    the holy avatar shall fight the demon,
the book of prophecies will knead a new day.

viii.
What pardon is possible here
in fields purchased with Judas' earnings
beyond the fertility of desert palms
red scented monkey-baits
homes for bees and concubines of the Pharoah
sires of African chieftains in Nubia
where songs were pyramids and architectonic music?
To what intervals shall we owe our reprieve?
    Love shall leaf these winter trees
    make visible home for wings
    and hearts tired in exile
    exploding the fertility of the acacia
       and the red-bottomed baboon.

ix.
Once upon a time a woman stood at her door
on the Greek Island of Hydra
crying; the moon came out
and she stopped crying.

x.

I will tell you my secret lies
my tented sorrow in Camel oases
waterholes dried in proper season,
golden palms in conspiratorial communion
with the rolling saharas of our history
when the sky gathered her death cloth
and rained pearls of beauty on us
in earthen huts of little food
while children brown as the ancient walls
caked in their murmuring corners
    tomorrow too the sun shall rise again!

Afro-American Beats

iv. *To Langston Hughes when He Walked*
Among Us in Kampala, 1962
To that gathering of wooden-headed boys
you came, pops, singing your jazz solos
in whiskied nights
black nativity for Rome, raisins in the sun
for Harlem, bagmen of black rebirth
beats of drums jive talk
and her daddy-o singing that song
"I wonder where I'm gonna die
being neither white nor black."
Your dusky rivers gurgling down your throat
watering fields for your soul
the rivers you've known
beneath slave ships
whip lashes

and the golden note
you heard the sweep of ancient rivers
and daddy-o you died in Harlem.

v. *To the Anonymous Brown-skinned Girl in Frisco*
I remember your face distinctly
haunting serenity glistening teeth
eyes the passion of centuries
we exchanged polite conversation
You took me in your Cadillac across town
to Oakland where pot-bellied papas
guard deserted storefronts,
there was the sting of tear gas
following the riots in the Berkeley air that May
broads and winos all over the place,
between periodic love making
you outlined your revolutionary dreams
your coming trip to Algiers,
the smell of afterlove
and spent weary pubic aroma
when at once the light shone from your dark beautiful soul
and I knew who you were.

vi.
Hold on there, the rag man
half-assed jiving mother
celebrant in rented tuxedo
barker at others' carnivals
for barren pennies you will vomit blood
and asphalt here in speaking to police dogs
and night sticks on the outskirts of Harlem;
my friend, pimp for downtown rich
limping from cudgel wounds
broken torso, black tooth jack-anapes

even the hairs in your ass-hole have been eaten by termites.
Remember what Malcolm said when you asked a dumb question?

vii. *Characteristic Leaders*
Charlie Parker, Coltrane
the true artists of a battered age
must take a trip; to draw cards
all true prophets must lose their voice;
for now the sanguine moon pale across my doorway
is singing in my bathroom
intricate fabrics woven in your trombonic voice
John the Baptist and the bird of paradise,
despised angel of infinite mercy
who made his nest in Newport
only to be despoiled. What happened
to the real voice of Miles before he abandoned
heavenly sounds for the vibrations of electricity
and jived doped rock bullshit?
When be-bop was born on hilly grounds,
these imitators were wriggling to the braying of donkeys
others were needed to keep their ears to earth
to hear the footfalls, and the beat, and crack
and vibes of mother's heart
across ten thousand years of our primal nakedness.

Etchings from My Mind

i.
Summer's sorrow surrogate heat
and the bark of magistrates
old men in ceremonial robes
dancers hoisted upon a hill
whirling on dead ants
to the cry of hornbills and cock calls.

ii.
An owl hooted in my memory tonight,
gaslit streets, the sacramento is passing.
Night falls slowly here.

iii.
That summer through Texas
Louisiana tropical imitations and land buyers stands
ranches, and oil magnates in ten gallon hats
bragging of their wealth and notches
on ancestral guns.

iv.
Through a snow haze
the road to Lockhaven, nightmare route 90 West
a hallucinatory promenade
to a farmhouse and a sentry dog,
a man seven feet carrying a ten-foot gun,
gas fumes from silver hills,
death in mountains, green murder baths
in single night motels.

v.
A festival of raw energy
and the sun shall shine in my valley.

vi.
Will this proscenium sorrow
feed the night hunger
at the festival of leaven bread
ears of corn my temples of sorrow?
Where is the harvest of my prayers?

across the bay come the morning
I shall wash this 37-year-old chill down
    and go home.

vii.
At the final hour comes the sorrow
pin pricks in summer's beginning;
alarms and bustles heard
over my grave; what carnival
now are they preparing? Plotting
my death again in cactus fields
and smoky barrooms; but my phoenix
flew to the cinnamon groves
and my grave is green on top.

Song of the bleeding throat
Death's outlet song of life. . . .
Whitman
(When Lilacs Last in the Dooryard Bloom'd)

My Father's Prayer

I dreamt again last night
One of those magic dreams of childhood.
It began, like my newest dream of maturing,
amicable enough for laughter,
exchange of small talk and destinies.
You spoke, as always, of how I am
the one who must resurrect
ancient days, raise again those
misty-glories of men and women
who linger vaguely in the memorials of the tribe.
    Then the dream changed,
    into a race we run, I
    as a boy running running
    away from home and perdition,
    and you the father chasing the son
    across hillocks, beyond monuments
    and graves, till the burial ground
    at graves-end where all stop.

My Uncle the Diviner—Chieftain

Another conversation, the godlike ram of sacrifices,
the only tree of the homestead now, occupant
and regent of an ancient honor house.
They all left you, the young ones,
the children you never had, the sons
you dreamt up filling your earth-space.
Your old age and our father's name,
roaring still unquenchable flames
through our land. I recall the day
the dark winds rose
whirling corn-cloths
leaves and fowl feathers
into the pyramidal household dream.
Then I came home. You stood on the compound
of our fallen homestead
nodding. A divination proceeds
from the diviner's good stomach.
Older memories and fire burning
over homesteads though fallen.
I was the messenger of that fire
the coming of that prophecy.

To Sika

Remember the Christmas
when on our way from Chelsea
you fell on pavements
broke a tooth and I was mute?
Your mother thought I was cruel,
but your fall hurt me
in that all of us,
your clansmen, fell on alien ground.
Remember the morning walks
to your nanny's
where you sulked and longed for home
the agony of flights and
the pain of separation looming
large like winter moons.
I knew I was the tempest
that will blast your youth
and misery of infancy.
Oh, I was the Abraham
sacrificing my Isaac
waiting in vain for the ram in the thicket
for dreams long forgotten under tropical suns.
But what could I have done?
Was I not aware of coming prophecies
   certainties
the final estrangement
prepared in secrecy
by the intervening gods of my household?
No. I was not seeking
an athanasia; how can I
The epilogue of my own long torment
And the sad prologue I dreamt you to be?

To Those Gone Ahead

To recall you all
demands the voice and memory
of brief madness beyond pain.
"The people gone that we loved"
is too flat Bill. I did not
know windswept places
without stars and moons,
I did not know wintry fevers
and venomous dog-nosed cold airs
slapping my face open-palmed
in hardened earth
under round yellow moons I never saw.
I recall them all, my mother's sister
She with the long tribe's mark
dying in her child's infancy;
my uncle Kundo chanting a dirge
till dawn in his armchair
into death's cold arms
at dawn.
My cousin Dede she whose memory
torments me like a lonely ghost
now rested beneath my house by the road
to direct us to ancient spots
of shrines and thunder-gods;
oh, she lyrical in my memory
like a biblical angel without
a tribe and a name.
What happened to that laughter
of childhood, the banana trees
watered by roots of bath
and birth waters flowing from

our ancient rivers
in dead groves?
Where did grandmother, a tall gazelle,
the only ancient tree when the hippo left,
pass with those interminable dirges
waiting for us to come home
with briars for her corn-wine
picked beneath harvest moons
that came home with us
from grandfather's farm far away?
And squirrels in palm groves
beneath graves covered in green
and broken pots
that cooked feast for long-forgotten
festivals in the village square.
Ah, and he the hippo himself
the force that reigned like
rains and thunders, inscrutable
as the clans' ways in those green days.
I remember the presentation
to the gods and ancestors
and the hippo's departure.
This is the parched grass's desire
for those gray waters
of rivers
far from the graveyards of the clan
the festival music fled,
low moans of slaughtered rams
tramplings of strangers
inherited the earth.
And I, Awoonor, the dropsied
seed from ancient loins
wander here where there is winter
birdsong and a yellow moon.

From *Night of My Blood* | 1971

I Heard a Bird Cry

There was a tree which dried in the desert
Birds came and built their nests on it
Funeral songs reached us on the village square
and our eyes were filled with tears
The singing voice which the gods gave me
has become the desert wind
Talk, my heart, talk,
Talk and let me hear,
And I will ask you how
How they avoided the sacred rams.

Your tears are running like a flooded river.
They are as bitter as the waters of the sea.
Why are your eyes so red?
Do you cover your head with your hands
And tremble like the orphan child by the
road-side?
I shall leave you
So that I can go to perform the rites for my gods
My, father's gods I left behind
Seven moons ago.

I shall weave new sisal ropes
And kill two white cocks
Whose blood will cleanse the stools.
The bitterness of your tears
Still lingers on my tongue
And your blood still clings to my cloth.

Do you remember that day
When I saw you

And asked whether you too
Believed in the resurrection of the living?
Remember that the green fields
Are waiting for the feet of the striving.

Hush, I heard a bird cry!
The winds of the storm have blown
destroying my hut
Goats came and did a war dance
On the fallen walls of my father's house
What happened before the vulture's head is naked?

Swear to me that you saw the widows
who beat the funeral drums
And put tears in the eyes of the orphans by
the road-side.

The path to the farm is long
Very, very long
The earthworm ate our new yams
And left the skins near the smithy shop
The smithy shop is on fire, my people
It is on fire
Remember the day the smithy shop caught fire
Remember you who are in the smithy shop.
Let me hear the funeral songs
Amidst the songs of the rebel gods
Marching to the dunghill
With fetish bells in their hands.

Hush! I heard a bird cry!

If you turn your neck
Look at the whole world
The heat and the restlessness

How drunken dogs are
Trampling precious things underfoot
And stray hyenas carry their loot
To the cleared patch in the forest,
Tears will gather in your eyes.
What has not happened before?
Though they said
The prince should not hasten for the stool
And the young leopard
Should not be in haste to walk
There are noises in the air.
The young leopard should stand up against
the tree.
And the prince should run for his father's stool.
The turbulent river becomes calm again
The desert river was dry
Before the harmattan came
And the storm wind does not
Frighten the eagle.

My people, where have you been
And there are tears in your eyes?
Your eyes are red like chewed kola
and you limp toward the fetish hut.
My people, what has happened
And you bear many cudgel wounds
and rope marks cover your naked bodies?
Wipe away your tears
And knock the door of the sacred hut
the gone-befores are waiting for you.

That day when they opened the sacred hut
And made pledges to the gone-befores
I was there.
They wound a cloth around my loins,

A fly-whisk in my right
And a calabash in my left hand,
I was there
When we pledged to the ancestors
And swore the oath
That you do not thirst
When your palm trees are prospering
That day we killed the sacred ram
And the thunder drums sounded
I was there.

I put down my white man's clothes
and rolled a cloth
To carry the ram's head
And go into the thunder house.
When you started the song
I sang it with you
My steps fell in
With the movement of your feet to the drums
I put my hand in the blood pot with you.

We sang new songs that day
It was the season of burning feet
Those who stood around the ring laughed
And said my feet had blundered
And our hands have lost the cunning of
the drums
We answered them, answered them
That the crow asked the vulture
You an uneatable bird
Why are you so full of your own importance?

I am the bird on the dunghill
The birds flew and left me behind.

My wings have not broken
But my joints are weak.
I too shall carry the fetish bell
And start toward the sacred hut
I will shout and call the ancestors
And tell them, tell them
That when the evil snake came
And bit me on Modui hillock[1]
I looked for a stick to kill it
But I never found one.

Hush! I heard a bird cry!

Look for a canoe for me
that I go home in it,
Look for it.
The lagoon waters are in storm
And the hippos are roaming

But I shall cross the river
And go beyond.

Where are the canoes?
I broke my paddle in the marshes
Mad dogs chased me
I left my cloth on the dunghill.
The fetish drums are beating from Ghost's Head[2]

---

1 Modui hillock: This is a hillock on the outskirts of Anyako, a town across the Keta
  Lagoon. This is the marking spot for Anyako's cemeteries since the town is virtually
  an island.
2 Ghost's head: The English translation of the name of an Ewe village in the Abor
  District.

And the priests are in trance.
My people, listen;
Listen and I will sing a song of sorrow.

My people and I went fishing
And met the evil god on the water.

Who are those coming
With their heads covered with velvet?
Maybe they are the moondwellers.
Tell them, tell them that the dog
Does not bear a child in public;
And the fowl-stealing hyena
Strikes only at night.

I heard the voice of a gun
I came to have a look
Who are those?
Who are those saying

They have surplus gunpowder
And so we cannot have peace?
I met Agodzo[3] by the road-side
A net on his shoulders
Complaining about the sea being bad these days
So his wives have run away to marry strangers.

It has happened again.
The swooping eagle does not give to its child.
So the child must turn a beggar in the
market place.
Brave warriors, come and hear

---

3   Agodzo: Everyman. Here, representative fisherman.

If the gun refuses to fire
Is it not the conservation of powder?
There is war in the land of the dead
And ghosts are doing a war dance
Marching with drums toward the land of
the living.
If I had known, if only I had known
I would have stayed at home.
I would not have gone to them
To ask what came to pass.

Listen, my countrymen, listen;
The bush fire burnt the bush
But did not touch the bush rope
Where has it been heard before?
Call my god of songs for me
That it will start a song for me.
I have a song to sing
I will sing it before death comes.
Let me be under the trees
And it will thunder
I will hear the voice of thunder.

We are on a stormy river
Rowing a boat to ghost's land.
The journey beyond is a long journey
That is why not one alone can make it.
The gone-befores will receive us
And give us water to drink,
Cool, cool water from the long pot.

We are on a journey
Somebody give me velvet
And I will put down the bark

And wear a gold chain
And walk a chiefly walk
For all to see.

Mad dogs came and bit people
In our house, in our own house.
We killed them, threw them on the dunghill
And ignored the linguist stick[4] when it came.

Hush! I heard a bird cry just now.

The heroes, where are the war heroes?
Did they smear themselves
With the blood of fowls
And are bellowing, bellowing,
Like wounded hippos?

If I had known.
I only I had known.
I would have stayed at home
to clear the bush
That crowded the sacred hut.
Then I would not have followed
The trancers to another land
Which cannot give me food to eat.
The swallow says
It is the harmattan wind
That chased him into the rafters of the rich.

Hush! I have just heard a bird cry.

---

4 Linguist stick: The symbol of the chief's authority. The linguist carries it to summon
   offenders to the chief's court.

They say it is in the night
When the monster terrorizes the people
They say it is in the night
When they gave birth to the evil child
And the smallpox god[5] walked the village lanes
Chasing with a stick
The dogs that barked at him.
They say it is in the night
When the big drums sounded
And evil-doers left their heads[6] by the riverside

They say it is in the night
When the white man deceived the chiefs
And took the young men to the battle front.

The day has broken
Men are still in their easy-chairs
Pipes in their mouths
Waiting for the women to return
They are still under the baobab tree
Telling tales of long-ago.

Under the trees, under the trees
I will be under the trees
And the rain will come and beat me.

5　Smallpox god: Sakpana, the Ewe god of smallpox, is reputed to be very powerful. He is referred to as the owner of the earth. At times he appears as a beggar covered with sores; at times as a rich man dressed in rich clothes. When he is a beggar, dogs chase and bark at him. Dogs are reputed to possess the power to see ghosts; they gather and bay at ghosts.

6　Left their heads: Refers to the punishment of execution meted out to serious criminals among the Anlos in the olden days in Anloga, the capital, and at a site near the lagoon.

When I spoke in public
They said I was drunk with gin.
My rich neighbor spoke in public
They said his wisdom is great
And the elders shook hands on it.
Weaver birds came and ravaged my corn-field.
I put my canoe on the river
I want to go beyond.

The river is wide, very wide
Then I saw two bamboos
Dancing on the wide, wide river.
A cock has laid an egg by the riverside
But a hawk came and snatched it.
What shall we do?

Some say we must cover our heads
With our hands, and burst into tears.
But I will not cry.
I shall put on my stinking cloth
And speak in the market place.
If the elders protest
I shall ask them, ask them,
When the sea was sterile
And the poor died of hunger on Modui hillock
Where were you?

A woman in pain of labor
Came and delivered a child on the dunghill
And named it "they don't know poverty."
Tell Agonyo[7] that I am coming

---

7   Agonyo: Everyman. Here, a member of the poet's audience.

The singing voice I have,
I have it from the gods
Those who cannot bear my songs,
Let them patch their ear holes with clay.

Where has it been heard before
That a snake bit a child
In front of its own mother?

The rain that beat me yesterday
Has become the flood water
That ravaged the rich people's corn-barns.
Let the tree die, and the branches remain.
The royal palm said he does not talk in vain
It is the whirlwind that provokes him.

Ask the fisherman, ask them,
When they went to sea,
What did they see?

Listen, and I shall sing a song of sorrow.
Some day, by some rivers
I shall sit down among the elephant grass
And listen to the roar of the estuary
Till the end of the world.
My people, listen to my song
The drunken dogs you saw yesterday
They have returned.
The rich men prepared a goat feast,
To this they invited all men,
But if you go without the white man's coat
You will be told the truth
That your grandfather lived on a tree.
That is how it has become.

When the church mothers waved palm branches
And sang of Jerusalem the golden city
And hosannaed to the pentecostal spirit
They said that Christ's kindness is great
It is great, it is very great
And his mercy endureth for ever.

Stay with us, abide
You the everlasting merciful
That our corn should fill the cobs
And the sea retain her fertility.

They say, they say,
The day they release the prisoners
There will be blessings
And joy will be found again.
But who will release the prisoner?
And break the poor-man's hunger?
I was there when they released the prisoners.
I heard tears of anguish
And the agony of the hungry.
Let the earth keep silent
And let us hear.

The deaf ran home that day
Shaking their heads.

Hush! I heard a bird cry.

The vulture says, it says,
Because helpers are not there
That is why
I have shorn my head
Awaiting my funeral.

My heart, be at rest,
For the vultures that came,
Shaking the rafters of your house,
Have flown away, flown far away,
Toward the land of my forefathers.

It was in the season of burning feet,
And the feast is ready for us.

Night of My Blood

Did they whisper to us the miracle of time
Telling us over the dark waters
Where we came from? Did they
Call us unto themselves
With the story of time and beginning?
We sat in the shadow of our ancient trees
While the waters of the land washed
Washed against our hearts,
Cleansing, cleansing.
The purifier sat among us
In sackcloth and ashes,
Bearing on himself the burdens
of these people. He touched our
foreheads with the wine of sour corn
and sprinkled our feet
with the blood of the sacred ram
Whilst the baobab rained dew on our heads.
Comforter, where is your comforting?

With all our woes and our sins,

We walked from the beginning
toward the land of sunset.
We were a band of malefactors
And saints.
The purifier walked in our shadow
bearing the fly-whisk of his ancestors
for his task is not finished.
We stumbled through the briar bush
Consoling us, moved against the
passion of rest forever.
The touchstone of our journey
was the silent prayers of the purifier.
Then they asked whether the harvest
should be gathered. Who sowed the crops?
We do not know: the harvesters
We know them,
Them that howl all night in the lanes
returning every night from funerals
officiating at a million wakes.
Comforter, where is your comfort?

Gather us, gather us unto yourselves our fathers
That we may bear the terror of this journey.
Through the briar we stumble
bearing the million crucifixes of time.
Save us the terror of our burden
Cleanse us,
The desert trees howl with wind blows
for the waters had washed
The sand which tossed in eyes
that opened wide in night's darkness
and there was no light
save the silent prayers of the purifier
As we bore the million crosses

across the vastness of time.
Then they appeared, the owners of the land
Among them were the silent lovers
of night's long harmattans; questioners
at the fathers' weary court.
The girls bearing the flowers of the desert
Cinnamon and smeared with yellow pollen of the palm
Swaying through the earth beaten path fingers
pointed
singing songs we could not hear,
Tearing down the glories of a thousand shrines
and dancing.
Muddying the paved paths of the fathers
anointed, and the offering
they bore on the wooden plates
eyes glued on the offering plates
asking for the glory of the fathers' rebirth,
Their penance-prayer voicing
unto the fathers
Not asking for forgiveness.

We sat among the thistles of the desert
chewing the cactus freshened
by the tear-drops of long-ago.
Revelling howlers in time's garden
entering the forbidden grounds
stirring us from that sleep of time,
the bearers' head turned to sunset
trampling through desert sand
sang a song we could not
hear the music of.
It was the season of dry wind.

We are the sons of the land

bearing the terror of this journey
carrying the million crucifixes of time
Then we arrived by the river Mono.[1]
There we planted our bean plants
not to wait for the season of rain
We then were the harvesters
As we filled our barns
With the crops of the land
the strange land that gave us food to eat.
We opened wide our hearts
washed by the desert wind
for cleansing in the sacred river.
Our dreams were of a homeland
forever;
of a happier world.

Then we moved one day at dawn
carrying with us the remnants
of the feast of the Passover
stumbling through dusk dawn faded
daylight making for the forests of the south.
We marched through marsh and marsh
retrieving acres of white sand
inhabitants sea-crabs and the
nocturnal wail of the bull frog.
One day at noon[2] we arrived;

---

1   Mono: A river in Dahomey that marks an important state in the migratory journeys
    of the Ewes to their present homes from the upper regions of the Niger River. The
    Ewes as a people cover the territory that stretches between the Volta River in Ghana
    to the Mono in Dahomey.
2   One day at noon: This refers to the arrival of Togbui Wenya and the Anlo wing
    of the Ewes at their present home at Anloga on the sea coast in the southeastern
    corner of Ghana around the thirteenth century, or maybe earlier.

my people, we arrived.
The shiny shingles washed white
glistening like the sacred ram
sacrifice awaiting; the dart of surf thrusts
into the sides of the glistening ram
the foam topping the crest of the ram
The drums beat that day and many days
and still beat for the deliverance
from terror of the burden of that journey.

Stop the Death-Cry

Let all of you stop the death-cry
and let me hear.
It is home: I stood at death's door
and knocked throughout the night.
Have patience and I shall pay the debt.
Suppose I had someone
Someone who will call me the dove
and it will run and come to me.
I have something to say I want to say
But it surpasses saying.
The dove says it is the soft voice
Which takes gifts from elders.
The prepared-for war is never surprised
So have patience
and I will pay the debt.
I knocked at death's door all night.
It was only the sleeping crow who came.
"Go back and prepare your gods
and then come back."

So I left; I am seeking to prepare my gods.
I am seeking; I am seeking.

A Dirge

Tell them, tell it to them
That we the children of Ashiagbor's house[1]
Went to hunt; when we returned
Our guns were pointing to the earth,
We cannot say it; someone say it for us.
Our tears cannot fall.
We have no mouth to say it with.
We took the canoe, the canoe with the sandload
They say the hippo cannot overturn.
Our fathers, the hippo has overturned our canoe.
We come home
Our guns pointing to the earth.
Our mother, our dear mother,
Where are our tears, where are our tears?
Give us mouth to say it, our mother.
We are on our knees to you.
We are still on our knees.

---

1 Ashiagbor's house: The poet's mother's lineage was founded by an ancestor known
as Ashiagbor, who founded the stool. His maternal uncle is the present chief.

More Messages

I can go placing maggots on those fires
fanning the innerwards: I can sneak
along like the crawling beetles
Seeking through dust and dirt
the lonely miracle of redemption
I will sit by the roadside, breaking
the palm kernel, eating of the white
with the visiting mice
throwing the chaff to the easterly wind.
But will they let me go?
to nowhere where I can see
the sunlight fall on the green waters
and the ferrymen hurrying home
across with their heavy cargoes
of man flesh, child flesh, and woman flesh
To sit where I can gather my thoughts
and ask what I have done so long
why could I not eat with the elders
though my hands are washed clean in the salt river,
where they leave the paddles in the boat
to be carried by children of strangers.
Coming to that land that day
where sand strip covers childhood
and youth's memory; there was no storm
that did not speak to us
divining the end of our journey
promising that our palms shall prosper
and we shall not die by thirst
in the same land; where our fathers
lingered, ate from land and sea

drank the sweet of the ancient palms.
Will they let me go
and pick the curing herbs behind fallen huts
to make our cure, their cure?
is the guile of the forest animal
the lingering desire of every marksman
returning from futile hunt
beaten by desert rain and thistles
on his shoulder the limpid hare
and empty guns?
to hoe my own fields, plant my own corn
        to wait for rain to come?
The sacrifice of years awaiting
unlit fires, who to knowledge
prepare the feast of the resurrection
On many rivers' shores moved
the benevolent band, awaiting
        that season
The dawn second cock
split by the ears of rumor,
time to wash the new corn
ready for the grinders
light the family fire of flimsy twigs, prepare
the broom to sweep unto dunghills
Crimes that my fathers atoned for.
Some day, by some rivers!
We sang that song before
in the thousand seasons of good harvest
and full fish following our father's footprints
on the long shores.

They heard the thunder
from the great river's waves

as the road crossing snakes brood on rotten eggs
that our feet should move to make room
for an empty empty valley.
What happened with cries heard under trees
that many households are empty?
The powder house is fallen
So we cannot make war
For when the bulls are alive
could the cows perform weed.[1]

At the Gates

I do not know which god sent me,
to fall in the river and fall in the fire
these have failed me.
I move into the gates
demanding which war is it;
which war is it?
the dwellers in the gates
answer us; we will let that war come
they whom we followed to come
sons of our mothers and fathers
bearing upon our heads nothing
save the thunder that roars
who knows when evil matters will come.

---

1 Perform weed: Refers to the ceremony of widowhood performed for any woman
whose husband dies. It is an elaborate and at times a very painful ceremony since
tradition holds that the wife of a dead man bears some spiritual responsibility for
her husband's death. It involves expiation and cleansing.

Open the gates!
It is Akpabli Horsu[1] who sent me

Open the gates, my mother's children,
and let me enter.
Our thunder initiates have run amok
and we sleep in the desert land
not moving our feet.
We will sleep in the desert
guns in our hands we cannot fire
matchetes in our hands we cannot throw
the death of a man is not far away.
I will drink it; it is my god who gave it to me
I will drink this calabash
for it is God's gift to me.
Bachelor, never go too far[2]
for drummer boys will cook and let you eat.
Don't cry for me over
my daughter, death called her.
She is an offering of my heart.
The ram has not come to stay;
three days and it has gone.
Elders and chiefs, whom will you trust?
A snake has bitten my daughter and
whom will I trust?
Walk on gently; give me an offering

---

1 Akpabli Horsu: A famous Anlo warrior whose fame was widespread, and his name
is still sung in songs.
2 Bachelor, never go too far: The bachelor must not travel too far afield lest he suffers
from hunger. There are many jokes about the bachelor. A famous one is: "When
you hear a bachelor scream, do not be in a hurry to go to his aid, for it is either his
corn-flour bag or his beard which has caught fire."

that I will give to God
and he will be happy.

Uproot the yams you planted
for everything comes from God
it is an evil god who sent me
that for all I have done
I bear the magic of the singer that has come
I have no paddle, my wish,
to push my boat into the river.

The Dance

Come let us play at resolutions
let us work out the dance sequence
and the movements,
I your choreographer and your mover
You my dance and my movement.
No, no your hands must encircle the invisible
Your hips must harmonize with your feet.
Your chest must beat the time.
Yes, my dance, my movement,
They must tell the primal story
of birth waters, blood, umbilical cords
in defiance of moon marks at every turn.
Yes, my dance, my movement
They are not steps, no:
they are journeys, roads, avenues, boulevards
Dream boulevards of life incarnate.

Do Not Handle It

Death, do not handle it,
do not handle it.
It burns and freshens a living
stretched across expanses unknown
—to the beleaguered only—
she sat upon the worship stone
staring at the counting stick
marking the marks that marked
a long ago dream.
And as the drumbeat unfolds
her elemental nature
she clasps into her frigid womb
The worship and the marking totem.

All Men My Brothers

What shall we build, my brothers?
Temples and shrines and sacrificial slabs
whereon we will make our offerings
long rejected? On this body
marked by scars of long
known joys, let us build
another body in our own image.
As the whiplash sounds in the distance,
and army boots tramp on heavy pavements,
brother, another one has fallen,
another one, a stranger now
among all men my brothers.

Lament of the Silent Sisters

For Chris Okigbo, the well-known poet, killed in 1967 in the Nigerian civil war.

That night he came home, he came unto me
at the cold hour of the night
Smelling of corn wine in the dawn dew.
He stretched his hand and covered my forehead.
There was a moon beam sparking rays in particles.
The drummer boys had got themselves a goat.
The din was high in the wail of the harvest moon.
The flood was up gurgling through the fields
Birth waters swimming in floods of new blood.
He whispered my name in far echo
Sky-wailing into a million sounds
across my shores. His voice still bore
the sadness of the wanderer
To wail and die in a soft lonely echo
That echo I heard long ago
In the fall of night over my river,
In the distant rustle of reeds
At growth in the strength of my river.
Once upon an evening I heard it
Strung clear as the gong of the drummer boys
Bright burnished like the glint edge of
the paschal knife, ready anxious to cut
My cords and enter into my fields.
I was still a dream then
Carried by the flimsy whiffs
Of sweet scents borne aloft on the vision
Of my coming flood
That will bear me slowly and gently
Into his world of smiles and smells.
He was not very gentle with me

But I did not complain. The thrust
was hard and angry, severing the tiny cord
Shattering the closed gates of raffia
Gathering at its eye the reeds to feed my fishes.
My flood had not risen.

The canoe carried on the strength
Of his man rowed steep down my river
into a tumultuous eternity
Of green hills and mountains
That reeled and rolled to the river shore
To clasp and bear me away.

Then the floodgates opened
for justice to cleanse to purify
My evening of awakening
In the turbulence of his triumph
Into the bright evening of my rebirth.
The birth was tedious
The pangs were bitter
Into the bright evening I rushed
Crying I have found him I have found him.
He stood there rustling in the wind
The desire to go was written large upon his forehead.
I was not ready for his coming
I was not ready for his loneliness,
for his sad solitude against the rustling wind.
I was not ready for his entrance
Into my fields and shores of my river.
The entrance of raffia was closed
closed against his lonely solitude.

He stood beneath my entrance
In his approach I knew the steps he took
Like the departing Lazarus

Marching toward his grave.
I was not ready.
The flood was gurgling at his estuary
swimming within me birth waters
warmed by his coming. He was silent
mute against the rushing of the wind
to cry and die for his homeland.
My flood had not risen then.
Across my vastness he marched into the wind
his arms folded upon his chest,
his eyes searching for the gates
that will open his amulets
to snatch and wear his talisman of hope.
He marched into the wind
howling through door posts
to catch the boatman at the dawn point.
to ferry him across my river.
But I was not ready.

My hands stretched to cover his
in the darkness, to cover his eyes
in the agony of his solitude
to call him names I knew
to put the dressing from my womb
upon his cudgel scars,
to hold his hand in the clasp of nightfall.
He was mute; the wind had stopped rustling
He was erect like the totem pole of his household
He burned and blazed for an ending
Then I was ready. As he pierced my agony
with his cry, my river burst into flood.
My shores reeled and rolled
to the world's end, where they say
at the world's end the graves are green.

Hymn to My Dumb Earth

The rivers burst; the land was covered
with blood.
Everything comes from God.

By the cathedral
where the choir rehearses the *Messiah*
under the baton of Uncle Philip[1] who wrote
the anthem
is the museum run by the absent-minded scholar
facing the lunatic asylum squarely.
Give us this day our daily bread;
Hallowed be Thy name.
Slow, slow rock not the boat
baa baa black sheep have you any wool was the theme song
of the cantata[2] in which the patients fled
the hospital
for they said he operated every case including fever.
A man with hernia jumped over a six-foot wall
trekked eighty miles to his home town
to die.
The decree came from Caesar Augustus
that everyone must go to his hometown
to die.

The affairs of this world are like the

---

1 Uncle Phillip: Phillip Gbeho, who composed the Ghana national anthem.
2 Cantata: A popular dramatic form introduced by the Christian missions and still
performed in Eweland. It dramatizes mainly themes from the Bible, such as David
the Shepherd Boy, Nebuchadnezzar, Saul, and so on. It is drama accompanied by
choral music, which imitates the European opera.

chameleon feces
into which I have stepped.

He wrote the anthem Uncle Philip
One day in his lagoon home at home
for the nation. There were yells, Ashanti yells.
The politicians removed them,
that all may be one.
United we stand.
Divided we stand.
Everything comes from God.

Oh, someone,
Someone call the dove for me
and it will run to me;
keep quiet and I shall pay the debt.
My friend went to the U.N.
came home talking of the secret service.
Thelonius Monk played in the Village,
There were hymns sung
near the Arc de Triomphe
The fingers were those of Bud Powell
but the voice, the voice is Esau's.
In the upper room the Last Supper is laid
while the redeemed gangster[3] from Detroit
outlined his dream of salvation.
A hush fell upon the brethren
as they gathered after the fortieth day
in the upper room.
The road to Mecca they say

---

3   Redeemed gangster: Refers to the revolutionary Malcolm X, who was assassinated
    in February 1965 at the Audubon Theatre in Harlem. The poet met him in Accra
    in 1964.

lies through Harlem.
Bud,[4] our Bud, what killed you so young?
Everything comes from God.
The interpenetration of opposites,
The negation of negation,
The transformation of quantity into quality
and vice versa.[5]

There is a general booze-up
in the Park Caterina[6] tonight

A piano will collapse
as the workers sing "Evening In Moscow"[7]
across the bridge over the wide muddy Neva.[8]
Keep calm and I shall pay the debt.

He studied law in Dublin
His spectacles glinting
as he wrote decrees for every regime;
disqualification, forfeiture and seizure
of property, rumors and rumor-mongering;
wars and rumors of wars.
That is his talisman of hope.
Some comrades fled across the border
pursued by that which they were nourished by.

When I kept my mouth shut
am I in jail?
Keep mute, my friend,

---

4 Bud: Bud Powell, the well-known jazz pianist, whom the poet heard play at the
   Blue Note in Paris, summer 1961.
5 The interpenetration . . . vice-versa: These ideas arise from Marxist theory.
6 Park Caterina: A well-known amusement park in Leningrad.
7 "Evening in Moscow": A well-known Russian song.
8 Neva: The river Neva runs through Leningrad.

for everything comes from God.

They unfurled a banner near the mosque.
It was a dedication ceremony.
The Party secretary spoke
of victory, comrades.
There is victory for us
and the Party is Supreme!⁹

Arise ye starvelings from your slumber
Arise ye prisoners of want.

His uncle sits upon a bankrupt stool.
The sea is sterile.
The land has lost its fertility.
He cometh, strew his path with palms
for everything comes from God.

I have no sons to fire the guns
no daughters to wail
when I close my mouth
when I pass on
So I shall go beyond and forget.

They are singing obscene songs in the streets today.
Bud played his eyes closed
in the little club
cords of sorrow, of hyssop
soaked in rags for the Savior
to drink upon a Cross.

He drank it, for the lord did not
let the cup pass away.

---

9 The Party is Supreme: A well-known slogan of Nkrumah's C.P.P.

I will drink it;
My God gave it to me, this calabash;
I will drink it. The ram
did not come to stay.
Three days, and it is gone.

O, Come all ye faithless
bring your drums along.
You and I saw the beggar boy limp away
and we sighed for denying him.
Some day, by some rivers,
I shall sit down among the elephant grass,
beneath the hills of spice.
But will she dance again in our time?

By the souls of the heroes
beneath whose shades we live
and die[10] we pledge.

The Messiah will come again.
There is war in the land of the dead
Ghosts are doing a war dance.

Bud, Bud, play on, run your fingers through
for me; Let the people with smelly clothes
dance on.

What has not happened before?
An animal has caught me,
it has me in its claws
Someone, someone, save
Save me, someone

---

10 By the souls . . . we live and die: Words taken from the original version of the Ghana
    national anthem.

for I die.
What a wounded name.
At the Central Committee today
a vote was taken on democratic centralism.
It will be written next week
into the Constitution.
Everything comes from God.

Where are the Agbadza boys
Where are they? Did they pass away
with those songs and dance?
Many songs did we sing in Kleve.

Many more hymns shall we sing
to the pentecostal spirit,
to the paraclete, to grind our knives of war
ready for his coming,
The war of the new season
that is coming.

Left, right, left, right
The weak ones fall out
for their feet are tired.

The N.C.O.s took over the government
No, not here; Okigbo[11] fights unto the death

the fight to dare to dream
to build a dream
by the light of the paschal knife.
Everything comes from God.

So please be calm

---

11 Okigbo: The poet to whom "Lament of the Silent Sisters" is dedicated.

and I shall pay the debt.
Someone, someone call the dove
and he will run to me.
I have something to say;
it surpasses saying
But I will say it before death comes.

Under the trees, under the trees
I will be under the trees and . . .

Now letteth thou thy servant depart in peace.
So shall I sorrow in life's need?
I do not covet even a crown here
where my lord wore a crown of thorns
To seek for me a sweet life
where they nailed Him to a tree
To die the death of a sinner.

Were you there when they crucified my Lord?
O sinner, sometimes, sometimes
why don't you answer?
A man was brought into the O.P.D.[12]

His testicles smashed by a gun butt
A drunken soldier was arrested in Osu.
He confessed he did the testicle-smashing
The man was his uncle, son of
the family, the clan, the tribe,
the nation.
A new Constitution is drawn up
filled with webs of brilliant arguments
and quotations from Plato's *Republic*.
Africans know about such Grecian matters.

---

12 O.P.D.: Out Patients' Department.

Everything comes from God.
A noted chief, educated by the coffers
of an impoverished chiefdom, returned
from exile. He is a scholar, well read
in anthropology, sociology and in the cosmology
of collections of one guinea per head to build
a writer's and artist's home at Botianor[13]
by cultural activists.
He preached the era of the black man
conjured the ghost of Kwamina Ansah
who received the Portuguese in 1482
at Elmina where the old slave castle stands.
The African Personality!
Long Live the Party and the Leader!
The party is over, *les jeux son faites*!
Oui, vous voilà . . .
He is home now, sporting a big gold chain
sitting on boards and delimitation committees.
He swore he never had a card.
All of them were victims. He was forced
against his will. He was forced, my fathers.
He seeks exemption[14] from the decree.

Grant it, grant it, O Lord.
We're almost home
We are. Come along brother
Come along sister
Come along to ring those chiming bells.
The priests are in trance;
Their dreams were of a homeland;

---

13 Botianor: A little fishing village a few miles outside Accra on the Winneba road.

14 Seeks exemption: This refers to the disqualification decree of the government of the N.L.C. from which those who held political office under the Nkrumah government were asked to seek exemption.

in the cities they said the same prayers
and in the villages they made the same offerings.

For all things come from God.

We will not cry, nor cover our heads
with our hands, nor burst into tears,
for all things bright and beautiful
the Lord God made them all;
He clothed the lilies of the field
Even Solomon in his splendor
could not surpass them in splendor.
Pavilioned in splendor
the mantle the sea!
O son of man.
The brigade major held a conference;
fear death by guns.

Come let us play at resolves
along the pavements of the Holy Spirit Cathedral
The choir is rehearsing Handel's *Messiah*
The drums are stilled
And Bud is dead in the storm.

Will he not come again?

Blood knots tied in weaker vessels
drip through to nurture the fields
bring life to the acacia of the desert north
gnarled by the harmattan wind
in the season of gray light
of sand that tossed in eyes.
To feed blood to the hungry land
Sacrifice a cock, cleanse the stools
in the black waters of the Aka River
for all things come from God.

If I had known, if only I had known
I would have stayed at home.

Bud played the piano in Blue Note
That summer in Paris seven years ago
The howl of the mad shepherds broke in
from Folie Bergères; it was the Paris
of the gay bright summer seven years ago,
of the mad mad shepherds.
The Lord is my Shepherd.
I shall not want.
The love of motherland, oh motherland
we pledge to thee, the tenderness
of ancestral shrines rebuilt with raffia
cut by the banks of the Aka River.

and the rivers and the rivers,
the triumphant rivers of our dreams
of our birth waters gurgling in estuaries
to burst into the flood of our redemption.
The hippos are roaming.
Miadenyigba lōlōa.
Mado wonko de dzi
Le nye agbe blibo me
Nye magble wo di o.[15]

---

15 *Miadenyigba lōlōa* . . . : This is a stanza from a well-known anthem composed by
the late Evans Amegashie on the occasion of the fortieth anniversary of the reign
of the late Togbui Sri II, the Paramount Chief of the Anlos. It translates:

> Our beloved native land
> I shall always praise your name
> Throughout my entire lifetime
> I shall never forget thee.

I shall not forget thee.
If I forget thee, O Jerusalem,
Let my right hand forget her cunning.

An animal has me in its claws.
An animal has me.
So would I to the hills
Where springs are fresh;
I turn there to hear time's winged chariot
hurrying near
and see before me
Vast temples of inanities.

Everything comes from God.

Our Father who art in heaven.
do whatever that pleases you.

My soul is locked in alien songs.
I read a page from the great survey
of the English professor in Gower Street
And I am lost, lost to the world
and to me.

Everything comes from God.

Kites are flying toward the hills
gulls are returning to bird island.
Naked stand I before you.
Wipe away my tears, our mother,
that with a dried face I shall face my Maker
and ask Him, ask Him
that when the sea was sterile
and the poor died on Modui hillock

Where were you?
Master, if it is within your power
to be the oarsman for the fishermen,
Do it, do it.

The gourd went to the river
but never came back;
What shall we do?
Move your feet and let me pass
is better than an empty valley.

Adzo said she has refused.
She refused to marry me.
This dance is a matter for the hips,
the hips, the hips, the hips.
Thelonius, Gerry, Coleman[16] playing in the Village.

Abide with me
fast falls the evening tide
The darkness deepens
Lord with me abide . . .
Abide, stay you the everlasting merciful
And the orphan Bud died in the storm
of the triumphant river,
Change and decay in all around I see,
that will bear his sons away.

Go not gently into that dark night.
The gray dusk unwinds serpentlike
into the bright sharp midwinter summer.

---

16 Thelonius Monk, Gerry Mulligan, Coleman Hawkins: Well-known names in modern
    jazz.

The cold bites the earth of my ears venomous
and leaves the world to darkness
and to me.
Now fades . . .
Do not touch it, death.

Everything comes from God.

My cousin Dede[17] and I
We made wattles and palm leaves
into mats rested upon the matted earth
of mud dried by the receding lagoon
one harmattan noon many seasons ago
we cannot remember;
When dried we carried them over our heads
covers from the rain falling
in showers of sheets glistening
in the harmattan sun like new knives
fresh returned from the grinders.
She said an animal, any animal
delivered a child that day noon in the forest.
Waterstones fell, hail stones fell upon our land.
We raced to pick them up.
They melted.
We cried in the rain of the harmattan sun.

Everything comes from God.

Then my mother's only daughter died.
They wailed, beat their hands
over their mouths;

17 Dede: A cousin of the poet. She died in 1955.

Ao, when you go, where you are going
tell them tell the ancestors
that the trees in the fences were eaten by
termites,
Ao, my mother's only daughter,
An only child;
She alone, I alone,
Ao, Ao, Ao, Ao.

The beads she had
Were famished earthworms
When the sun dries the earth;
The yellow of ripening guava
The green of the medicinal avia[18]
the blue of the Lagosian dyer's[19] palm
The red the flame of the prize cock's horn—
All, all, all in the rainbow of our discontent.

I hear Thy welcome voice
I am coming Lord
Dear on, hold on
for I come.

Everything comes from God.

---

18 Avia: A well-known plant the leaves of which are used in divination and herbal
    medicine among the Ewes.
19 Lagosian dyer: Yoruba women are known throughout West Africa for their skill as
    cloth dyers.

They Do Not Sound for Me

Fetish drums sounding away
Many songs did the initiates begin
in Kleve.[1] Where are they?

Where are they? Where did they pass
with these songs
and drums and gongs and dance?
They were dancing the steps for the departed
Among the fields of thorns.
It was I who put my hand on
the infant drums in silence
that the adult drums should sound for me
that the song should sound for me
that the sound of feet in dance
should sound for me.
Sound for me to hear
Voice of Vedu[2] beside the weaver shop.

Gong and rattlers will sound for me
O, children of my mother, they do not sound.
The wind and the smoke machines
they sound in top voice hand beating
over mouth
revealing to me always
The messages of far away.

---

1   Kleve: A small forest south of Anyako, a source of firewood for the town. It is also
a fetish grove.
2   Vedu: He is a first cousin of the poet and is a *heno*, or "traditional poet." He leads
a group of drummers and dancers and has a sizeable reputation as a poet in Ewe.

From *Rediscovery
and Other Poems*

1964

My God of Songs Was Ill

Go and tell them that I crossed the river
While the canoes were still empty
And the boatman had gone away.
My god of songs was ill
And I was taking him to be cured.
When I went the fetish priest was away
So I waited outside the hut
My god of songs was groaning
Crying.
I gathered courage
I knocked on the fetish hut
And the cure god said in my tongue
"Come in with your backside"
So I walked in with my backside
With my god of songs crying on my head
I placed him on the stool.
Then the bells rang and my name was called thrice
My god groaned amidst the many voices
The cure god said I had violated my god
"Take him to your father's gods."
But before they opened the hut
My god burst into songs, new strong songs
That I am still singing with him.

The Sea Eats the Land at Home

At home the sea is in the town,
Running in and out of the cooking places,
Collecting the firewood from the hearths
And sending it back at night;
The sea eats the land at home.
It came one day at the dead of night,
Destroying the cement walls,
And carried away the fowls,
The cooking pots and the ladles,
The sea eats the land at home.
It is a sad thing to hear the wails,
And the mourning shouts of the women,
Calling on all the gods they worship,
To protect them from the angry sea.
Aku stood outside where her cooking pot stood,
With her two children shivering from the cold.
Her hand on her breast,
Weeping mournfully.
Her ancestors have neglected her.
It was a cold Sunday morning,
The storm was raging,
Goats and fowls were struggling in the water,
The angry water of the cruel sea;
The lap-lapping of the dark water at the shore,
And above the sobs and the deep and low moans
Was the eternal hum of the sea.
It has taken away their belongings.
Abla has lost the trinkets which
Were her dowry and her joy,
In the sea that eats the land at home,
Eats the whole land at home.

The Cathedral

On this dirty patch
a tree once stood
shedding incense on the infant corn;
its boughs stretched across a heaven
brightened by the last fires of a tribe.
They sent surveyors and builders
who cut that tree
planting in its place
a huge senseless cathedral of doom.

What Song Shall We Sing

Shall we jump and clutch at the stars
Singing hosannas?
Shall we sing the flesh peeling songs
Of goose-pimples,
Or shall we sing the new songs
That are on the lips of the street boys?
What song shall we sing?

The drums are beating
          and beating
Man of huge testicles draw away.
          draw away, draw away.
Peal on, peal on
Peal on and let the people with dirty clothes dance on.
Here come the travelers with new songs
Let us learn the new songs from afar.

We Have Found a New Land

The smart professionals in three piece
Sweating away their humanity in driblets
And wiping the blood from their brow
  We have found a new land
  This side of eternity
  Where our blackness does not matter
  And our songs are dying on our lips.
Standing at hell-gate you watch those who seek admission
Still the familiar faces that watched and gave you up
As the one who had let the side down,
"Come on, old boy, you cannot dress like that."
And tears well in my eyes for them
Those who want to be seen in the best company
Have abjured the magic of being themselves
And in the new land we have found
The water is drying from the towel
Our songs are dead and we sell them dead to the other side.
Reaching for the Stars we stop at the house of the Moon
And pause to relearn the wisdom of our fathers.

The Anvil and the Hammer

Caught between the anvil and the hammer
In the forging house of a new life,
Transforming the pangs that delivered me
Into the joy of new songs
The trappings of the past, tender and tenuous
Woven with the fiber of sisal and

Washed in the blood of the goat in the fetish hut
Are laced with flimsy glories of paved streets.
The jargon of a new dialectic comes with the
Charisma of the perpetual search on the outlaw's hill.
Sew the old days for us, our fathers,
That we can wear them under our new garment,
After we have washed ourselves in
The whirlpool of the many rivers' estuary.
We hear their songs and rumors every day
Determined to ignore these we use snatches from their tunes,
Make ourselves new flags and anthems
While we lift high the banner of the land
And listen to reverberation of our songs
In the splash and moan of the sea.

Rediscovery

When our tears are dry on the shore
and the fishermen carry their nets home
and the seagulls return to bird island
and the laughter of the children recedes at night,
there shall still linger here the communion we forged,
the feast of oneness which we partook of.
There shall still be the eternal gateman
Who will close the cemetery doors
And send the late mourners away.
It cannot be the music we heard that night
That still lingers in the chambers of memory.
It is the new chorus of our forgotten comrades
And the halleluyahs of our second selves.

The Weaver Bird

The weaver bird built in our house
And laid its eggs on our only tree.
We did not want to send it away.
We watched the building of the nest
And supervised the egg-laying.
And the weaver returned in the guise of the owner.
Preaching salvation to us that owned the house.
They say it came from the west
Where the storms at sea had felled the gulls
And the fishers dried their nets by lantern light.
Its sermon is the divination of ourselves
And our new horizon limits at its nest.
But we cannot join the prayers and answers of the
    communicants.
We look for new homes every day,
For new altars we strive to rebuild
The old shrines defiled by the weaver's excrement.

The Purification

The sea-god has deserted the shore
And the day-long net lands with catches of weed
Then the storm came
Chastening the birth bowels and cords of sacraments.
We stood on the shore and watched you sail
To the roar of the sea and the priest's bell.
They didn't forget to place the sacrificial cow
On the bow of the storm-experienced canoe

Anipaye the fish[1], I shall stay at the net's end
While you go down.
While you go down.
I shall be under the tree
And the rains will come and beat me
And the tree will die and leave its branches
And Anipaye you will go down.
Then you were lost where earth and sea met
And we didn't know what happened.
The sea roared and ran around
Like the madman at moonrise.[2]
But it stopped, it suddenly stopped.
The cow and Anipaye had gone down.

The Gone Locusts

I saw tree tops from the desert land
And wished I could pluck the green leaves and make myself
    a hut.
I sat there and watched the locusts
From the east come in clouds;
And then the green tops of the trees were no more.
Then I and the trees and the gone locusts became the desert
    dwellers.
Yet I shall be under the trees

---

1   Anipaye: A very common silvery fish in West African waters.
2   Madman at moonrise: The moon is traditionally believed to have an effect on the
madman. This effect is more noticeable with the rise of the new moon. The mad
person usually gathers rags and all kinds of rubbish when his madness comes on,
just like the sea, and deposits them again in the moment of calm.

And the rains will come and beat me.
I shall wish for the return
Of the sowing season
In which the farmer
Will remember his harvest.

Songs of Sorrow

I.

Dzogbese Lisa has treated me thus
It has led me among the sharps of the forest
Returning is not possible
And going forward is a great difficulty
The affairs of this world are like the chameleon feces
Into which I have stepped
When I clean it cannot go.[1]

I am on the world's extreme corner,
I am not sitting in the row with the eminent
But those who are lucky
Sit in the middle and forget
I am on the world's extreme corner
I can only go beyond and forget.

My people, I have been somewhere
If I turn here, the rain beats me
If I turn there the sun burns me
The firewood of this world

---

1   Colloquial: It (the feces) will not go (come off).

Is for only those who can take heart
That is why not all can gather it.
The world is not good for anybody
But you are so happy with your fate;
Alas! The travelers are back
All covered with debt.

II.
Something has happened to me
The things so great that I cannot weep;
I have no sons to fire the gun when I die
And no daughters to wail when I close my mouth
I have wandered on the wilderness
The great wilderness men call life
The rain has beaten me,
And the sharp stumps cut as keen as knives
I shall go beyond and rest.
I have no kin and no brother,
Death has made war upon our house;

And Kpeti's great household is no more,
Only the broken fence stands;
And those who dared not look in his face
Have come out as men.
How well their pride is with them.
Let those gone before take note
They have treated their offspring badly.
What is the wailing for?
Somebody is dead. Agosu himself
Alas! A snake has bitten me
My right arm is broken,
And the tree on which I lean is fallen.

Agosi if you go tell them,

Tell Nyidevu, Kpeti, and Kove
That they have done us evil;
Tell them their house is falling
And the trees in the fence
Have been eaten by termites;
That the martels curse them.
Ask them why they idle there
While we suffer, and eat sand.
And the crow and the vulture
Hover always above our broken fences
And strangers walk over our portion.

From *This Earth, My Brother:*
An Allegorical Tale of Africa   1971

The Making of a New Nation

Bricks cement mortars pounding. A nation is building. Fartfilled respectable people toiling in moth-eaten files to continue where the colonialists and imperialists left off.

The poor are sleeping the sleep of the hungry under the nims. Benevolent one, thou who hast asked us to do your bidding, thou who has begged us with tears in your eyes and soot on your face, Follow my laws, my children, follow my laws for I am the one who brought you from the dust of degradation. . . .

Woman, behold thy son; son, behold thy mother. This revolting malevolence is thy mother. She begat thee from her womb after a pregnancy of a hundred and thirteen years. She begat thee after a long parturition she begat you into her dust, and you woke up after the eighth day screaming on a dunghill.

You crawl through the dunghill of Nima unto the blue hills of smoke to catch the infinite immeasurable bliss to say to the dancers on the hills of spice, lift up your clothes for the nation is yours, the land has come back. The yoke has been smashed by the knights of valor, the corridors are cleared for new feet to walk through.

Then they grasp the strength and energy and freedom of the spirit not to make the infinite movement of resignation but to make the paraclete their own, to make the fire their own, to make the tongues that descended upon them that dark night lit by torches from a million and a million hands their own.

In the hush hour of birth came the songs, the siren of joy and the land took on new color, as voices raised a new chorus to the sky.

And no one stood alone in that hour. Strangers hugged one another, those who spoke not the same tongue embraced one another in the magic hour of faith and renewal of faith.

I am able by my own strength to renounce everything, and then to find peace and repose in pain. . . .

Home is my desolation, home is my anguish, home is my drink of hyssop and tears. Where is home?

My search for repose in pain is not an act of faith. It is an act of worship for fallen gods, gods burned out by colonial district commissioners armed with a governor's order-in-council: that all false gods among the pagan Gold Coast African should be destroyed; troops—an adequate number in order not to provoke uprisings and only where persuasion fails—destroy gods by persuasion—maybe destroyed with maximum precaution.

Our father who art in heaven, do whatever pleases you. The menace of a raging tooth is eliminated by extraction, if necessary by force of arms meaning by persuasion.

So gods must be exiled, driven out of the land for failure, wicked unwarrantable failure. We had placed our hopes in them. They must go into exile. We don't care where. But they must leave the land which they have desecrated with their foul excrement.

Despair and die.

The self-illumination that comes of the losing of senses in a twilight field of new sensations and a new physical dimension will provide the avenue of final immersion, of the incessant and immutable necessity to be aware of our strength. Then, and only then, shall we assume the strength of lions, and stalk the spoor of him our Maker among the Creator's ignoble herd . . . .

After the firing of the muskets on the famous twenty-fourth, the Party activists were rounded up. Some were screaming in tears and supplication, some marched with their heads bowed. Then they were beaten, on television only. They were not beaten in reality. The world was told it was a bloodless takeover. Some women have not seen their husbands since, except those who saw their husbands in army uniforms driving Mercedes 250 top speed toward the castle. The same castle where the slave ship anchored, and received their cargoes through the tunnels to the Americas. . . .

On the Liberty Arch the words are inscribed, "Freedom and Justice." The darkness of the black star lies in its square where immerse appropriations are made to increase the striking force of the army of a starving, naked, and diseased nation to march and wear its boots newly received from England under certificates of urgency—judging the state of depletion of the national coffers—the one who left stole all the money, the bastard, the b.f.—new epaulettes, new strings, new crowns for newly appointed generals and brigadiers, and uniforms for latrine carriers.

Fear death by guns.

From *Comes the Voyager at Last:*
A Tale of Return to Africa 1992

Festival of Oneness

On the dawn of the fifth day after the lull and the calm of the inconsolable sea, the skies burst open in a fury of thunder and storm. Our craft, which once had looked formidably large even in the face of the ocean, was borne on the waves of the howling winds, whipped and lashed in an unwarned fury that raged for days. In our holds, already reduced in spirit and flesh by the agony of our fate, on this lachrymose graveyard afloat, we were ready to step cold-blooded into this new torment which could yet be our salvation. We hear the song, prohibitive, its voice slashed and barbed, wounded beyond time. All over, in the vortex of the darkness, were the bodies of our companions paralyzed by the total mystery of our fate. The craft rose and fell, caught in the spasm of dying in the throes of the beginning, crashing and crushing us as we lay in our captive chains. For days we lay in our vomits, in the pungent smell of the sick and the dying in that overwhelming scent of our ultimate humanity.

The storm abated on the tenth day. It abandoned us as suddenly as it came. We lay spent and weary. It looked as if the once defeated sun had appeared, invisible to us in our prison, but emitting even into the dungeon its light and benevolence, restoring for us a brightening hope. On that first day of calm, some of our captors who themselves must have been sick, appeared to check our numbers and to reassure themselves of the safety of their goods. The dead were removed. They returned to the upper world abandoning us, the survivors, once again to our calamitous dreams.

Day after day in the lethargy of this calmness, the voyager was coming, brought along by more than chance, the ocean, its peopled seas, and the inviolable sun. Soon, soon, he would be home . . . . . .

. . . . *THE LANDSCAPE WAS THAT ONE I KNEW* in the pri-
meval clarity of the absence of time, the sacred moments of pain and
joy, in the combined miracle of birth and death, in the only reality
of my body fate and destiny. It was a sweeping valley, verdant, clotted
here and there by the tallest trees of creation. The birds, led by the
Bird, were a flock of dazzling arcs and colors circling the tallest trees.
Underneath, upon the earth, the man was finishing the last offering,
preparing the offals for the altar on the lowest hill beneath the tree.
It is this that the birds were hovering over, awaiting it seemed, their
summons to partake of the sacrifice. They carried the woman, laid her
on the earth, her face shining with a power that was indescribable. Her
beads were loose on her body. She was limp. Her eyes were glazed. She
was borne by two tall men in loin clothes. The moon, fiercely red, was
suspended. Through the valley beneath the altar mountain flowed the
river, the sister of the ocean whose rumble I heard beyond the hills.
From here, I received the intimate knowledge of the mosaic structure
of my first contact with infinity. So the invulnerable arena of my soul
was part of the landscape, of the magical leaping feat of the Fish, the
purest witness to my primordial pain. I myself took on the wings of the
Bird, the fins of the Fish, the towering height of the Tree, the eternity
of the River and the depth of the Ocean. I was the Man, the Woman,
and the Child on the voyage between earth and sky, in the thrill of the
perilous flight of all things. But my solitude was adamant, as I hung
between life and death, death and sky, treading my assumptions and
distinct disabilities underfoot. I was the invincible essence of the rising
phoenix, of the undying animal of all our humanity. Here the dead
lily of the vanquished desert was blooming again; alive again were the
creepers and lichens of the inconsolable forest, the flying corridors of
heaven, the brown elephant grass of the savanna, the nurturing home
of the elemental seed. This conglomerate, this ultimate was spelt by the
vision of the girl among the scents, the excitation of the birds, the joy
of the fishes and the ecstasy of the wild lilies. The suspended and the
preoccupied moon, destitute passion of my rebirth, was the cleansing
force washing away the hate and calamity I once bore.

I alighted now at the last edge of the valley. The music that had once become a slow monotone had changed into a clanging celebrative din of drums, cymbals, bass guitars, trombones, and the quivering voices of shivering trumpets. Then, as if in response to the music's call, the whole valley burst into life. There poured into it from nowhere a host of men, women, children, and flocks of birds that darkened the face of the moon, trailed by stars across the heavens shooting at quick intervals into the valley. The people were of all the colors of the earth, pale, pink, red, brown, black, Europeans, Jews, Asians, Africans, each group in its colorful clothes. Among them were some with heads reaching to the skies, some whose feet were turned inside out, some were dwarfs whose nearness to the earth hardly afforded them somersaulting room. Some were musicians playing all the instruments of the earth in a cacophonous din making the type of music the poet called the tumult of a mighty harmony that could frighten the deaf. There were drummers, flutists, oboists, guitarists, xylophonists, trumpeters. Then followed an army of magicians, jugglers, acrobats, and sorcerers in whose hands all things were given birth and death, men who held the sky and the earth in lingering parley, released with their mouth the hidden essence of all things, restoring the unity of ALL by the power of the WORD. And then came the gods and kings, the secret guardians of the universe whose brothers were the Bird, the Tree, the Mountain, the River, and the Ocean. They flew like the wind on galloping horses across the valley, cried like the howling thunder, destroyer and unifier. At the last tip came the infants accompanied by the wild beasts the lion, the leopard, the tiger, the wolf, the hyena, led by the smallest child on their way to the festival.

Then I heard my name called thrice in the mouth of thundering cannons, poignant. I stepped out behind the procession toward the mountain altar. But my walk was a flight. I was being borne to where the woman lay. Through the hosts, through the animals whose smells I bore in my nostrils, through the midst of the musicians and their deafening sounds, through the vortex of the purifying fire I emerged, swooping now, settling over the universe, resting by the side of my love. Then the children came forward and touched me, caressed me with their infant hands. They were of all colors as the men and women. They breathed upon me their infant breaths exuding the primal scent of sweet barks out in the winter. Then the animals came to where we lay, nuzzling and rubbing their snouts against my face and forehead. Then the gods and the king, the meekest of them all, benevolence emanating from their countenances. After this interminable libation in which I was bathed in tears, sweat, saliva, and the passionate incenses from the mouths of the sorcerers, the children, and the gods, we were left alone on the mountain, she and I. The old man was bending over us; his breath sweet, his eyes the brown color of the earth. She to whom I was summoned was sitting upon the reed mat on the altar. Her hands were rested upon my brow. The old man spoke, now, he chanted a prayer. The valley was aglow with a bright incandescent light. The lingering mourning hymn had gone. The music was ended. Then I saw him retreating over the tallest hill, going. She and I were alone.

And I knew it was more than that, it was infinitely more than that.

AN EPILOGUE

Kofi Awoonor

About roots, I will like to offer you the following.

I was born seventy-eight years ago in a small farming village of Wheta, two miles from the Keta Lagoon and about six miles from the sea. The area is characterized by creeks, a little river called Aka, marshland, and an extensive forest that no longer exists thanks to the government-sponsored rice farm project built with the help of the Soviet Union and later China. When I was a boy, the area was teeming with wildlife: antelopes, warthogs, and a large variety of waterfowl. Today, only the waterfowl, in a reduced number, visit from I know not where. The animals are all gone.

My mother was the first child of a chief, Nyidevu Besa of the division of Asiyo, a noted elder and a successful farmer. My father came from Anyako, about ten miles away, and had settled in the town of Dzodze, where he practiced the trade he learned, tailoring. He had about four years of education in the famous Bremen Presbyterian Mission School up till 1920 or so when his father put him away together with his mother for reasons that are still locked in the past. He went with his mother to Anyako where he fished and learned tailoring, emigrating with his uncle in 1930 to the town of Dzodze, a growing agricultural trading town over twenty miles away. It was here he met, in 1934, my mother who went regularly to the market there to sell farm produce. My mother had never been to school, and because my father came from a more "Europeanized" background, he had my mother baptized into the Presbyterian Church. I grew up on the lap of my grandmother Afedomeshi, a great singer of dirge songs and a hardworking and beautiful woman who died in 1946 or so.

I grew up in the rural towns of Wheta, Dzodze, and Keta, our "big" commercial and fishing town of about two thousand people. I went to elementary school first at the Roman Catholic Mission School at Dzodze from 1939 to 1943. Then I transferred to the Keta Bremem Mission School, my father's old school, founded by the church to which his paternal grandfather gave land in 1847.

I grew up in a typical African community of relatives, aunts, uncles, some of whom came from as far afield as Togo (from where, before the boundaries, my father's father's mother came). Though there was Christianity, our family possessed a major thunder shrine at Wheta, and my maternal relatives took very little interest in the European's religion. Their world was my real world of consciousness, of growth. It was formed in mysteries about life; it had to do with an invisible living phenomena that pertained to everyday existence. I do not rationalize this world now because I have returned to it, to the underlying energy that sustains it. The principle that I believe was at its base was *continuity,* for as our people say, *eka xoxoawo nue wogbea yeyeawo do*: "we weave the new ropes where the old ones left off."

There is in this concept the fundamental unity, of time and place, with the people always the actors; the terrain and the time reveal the nature of the activities of my people, for in the need for continuity is stressed the principle of survival.

The magical and mysterious relationships defining only the very simple and the mundane have, beyond time and place, their anchorage in *words*. Our people say the mouth that eats salt cannot utter falsehood. For the mouth is the source of sacred words, of oaths, promises, prayer, and assertions of our *being*, presence, affirmation. This is the source of my poetry, the origin of my commitment—the magic of the word in the true poetic sense. Its vitality, its energy, means living and life giving. And that is what the tradition of poetry among my people has always meant. It had as its fundamental thrust the celebration of living itself against a background of suffering, children dying at birth, mothers dying at childbirth, children not reaching the age of ten, and old men and women, survivors all, left to tend the homesteads. Survival in this situation was more than a matter of hope. It was anchored in faith, belief, and certainty that life is a cyclical process; we fulfill our turn with drums, laughter, and tears, and pass on inevitably to our ancestorhood, to sustain those we leave behind on this wayside farm we call life.

SOURCE ACKNOWLEDGMENTS

Comes the Voyager at Last: A Tale of Return to Africa. Trenton NJ: Africa
    World Press, 1992.
"Herding the Lost Lambs." Unpublished manuscript, last modified 2013.
The House by the Sea. Greenfield Center NY: Greenfield Review Press,
    1978.
Latin American and Caribbean Notebook. Trenton NJ: Africa World
    Press, 1992.
Night of My Blood. Garden City NY: Doubleday, 1971.
Ride Me, Memory. Greenfield Center NY: Greenfield Review Press, 1973.
Rediscovery, and Other Poems. Ibadan, Nigeria: Mbari Publications,
    1964.
This Earth, My Brother: An Allegorical Tale of Africa. Garden City NY:
    Doubleday, 1971.
Until the Morning After: Selected Poems, 1963-1985. Greenfield Center
    NY: Greenfield Review Press, 1987.

IN THE AFRICAN POETRY BOOK SERIES

The Promise of Hope:
New and Selected Poems, 1964–2013
Kofi Awoonor
Edited and with an introduction
by Kofi Anyidoho

Madman at Kilifi
Clifton Gachagua

Seven New Generation African Poets:
A Chapbook boxed set
Edited by Kwame Dawes and
Chris Abani

To order or obtain more information on
these or other University of Nebraska Press
titles, visit www.nebraskapress.unl.edu.